SCHOLASTIC

MY FIRST BILINGUAL
Little Readers

by Deborah Schecter

NEW YORK • TORONTO • LONDON • AUCKLAND • SYDNEY
MEXICO CITY • NEW DELHI • HONG KONG • BUENOS AIRES

Teaching *Resources*

*In memory
of Maggie*

Cover design by Maria Lilja

Interior design by Sydney Wright

Illustrations by Anne Kennedy
except pages 6 and 13 by James Graham Hale, and page 9 by Rusty Fletcher

Spanish translation by Jorge Dominguez

ISBN: 0-439-70069-8
Copyright © 2005 by Deborah Schecter
Published by Scholastic Inc.
All rights reserved.
Printed in the U.S.A.

8 9 10   40   22 21 20

Contents

Introduction 4

Tips for Using
My First Bilingual Little Readers 4

How to Make the Little Readers 5

Connections to the
Language Arts Standards 6

Extending the Books 6

School Days
Días de escuela

Hurry Up! Hurry Up!
¡De prisa! ¡De prisa! 15

I Like School!
¡Me gusta la escuela! 17

Class Pets
Las mascotas de la clase 19

Shapes for Lunch
Figuras para el almuerzo 21

Fun at the Playground
A divertirse en el parque infantil 23

Friends, Friends, Friends
Amigos, amigos, amigos

What Do I Need?
¿Qué necesito? 25

Birthday Surprise
Sorpresa de cumpleaños 27

Fun With Mud
A divertirse en el barro 29

Where Is Petey?
¿Dónde está Pedrito? 31

Sweet Treat
Algo muy rico 33

What's in My World?
¿Qué hay en mi mundo?

What Shines?
¿Qué brilla? 35

I Like Stripes
Me gustan las rayas 37

What Is Red?
¿Qué es rojo? 39

Bubbles!
¡Burbujas! 41

What Can I See?
¿Qué veo? 43

Around the Seasons
En las estaciones

Cold Rose
Rosa tiene frío 45

Winter Is Here
Llegó el invierno 47

Almost Spring
Ya casi es primavera 49

When Night Comes
Cuando cae la noche 51

Hello, Beach
Hola, playa 53

All About Me
Todo sobre mí

I Can Draw!
¡Puedo dibujar! 55

Hide and Seek
A las escondidas 57

Hats, Hats, Hats
Sombreros, sombreros, sombreros 59

What Is for Supper?
¿Qué vamos a cenar? 61

Look What I Found!
¡Mira lo que encontré! 63

Introduction

Welcome to *My First Bilingual Little Readers*, a collection of 25 little books written in English and Spanish to correlate to Guided Reading Level A, and designed to support children at the emergent stage of reading. The stories feature a variety of familiar and favorite topics that children will enjoy reading about, such as preparing for the first day of school, playing with friends, the outdoor world, seasonal changes—and themselves! *My First Bilingual Little Readers* will help children get a great start in reading as they learn to love to read!

My First Bilingual Little Readers include the following features:

* Consistent text placement on each page—English at the top and Spanish at the bottom
* One to two lines of text per page
* Short sentences with repetitive sentence structure
* Repeated and recognizable high-frequency sight words
* Rhyming text to build recognition of word families and other phonics skills
* Engaging illustrations that closely match the text
* Familiar story themes that connect to children's experiences and interests

☆ Tips for Using *My First Bilingual Little Readers* ☆

Before Reading Take a picture walk through the book with children and invite them to tell what they think the book will be about, make connections to their own experiences, and identify familiar and unfamiliar words. Discuss strategies children can use to decode unfamiliar words, such as finding beginning or ending sounds, breaking the word into parts, and using picture clues. Provide background for any concepts in the book that might be unfamiliar to children.

During Reading Let children read the book aloud softly as you listen in. Help children use problem-solving strategies when they encounter unfamiliar words. You can offer support and encouragement without interrupting the flow of their reading.

To assess children's decoding skills, take a running record as they read, noting the problem-solving strategies used by each child as well as strengths and needs. Use these questions as a guide:

☑ Do children follow the print with their eyes (indicating greater fluency) or use their fingers to follow the words?

☑ Do they recognize most words or use their knowledge of sound-spelling relationships to decode unfamiliar ones?

☑ How well do children use context clues from surrounding words and pictures to figure out the meaning of new words?

☑ Do they self-correct by rereading to pronounce difficult words or to improve expression?

☑ Do children use appropriate inflections when they encounter question marks, and interpret other punctuation correctly?

How to Make the Little Readers

Follow these steps to copy and put together the mini-books:

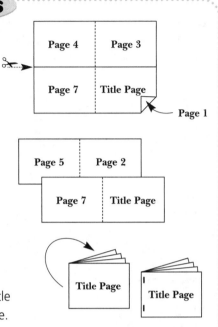

1 Remove the mini-book pages along the perforated lines. Make a double-sided copy on 8 ½- by 11-inch paper.

2 Cut the page in half along the solid line.

3 Place page 2 behind the title page.

4 Fold the pages in half along the dotted line. Check to be sure that the pages are in the proper order, and then staple them together along the book's spine.

NOTE: If you cannot make double-sided copies, you can photocopy single-sided copies of each page, cut apart the mini-book pages, and stack them together in order, with the title page on top. Staple the pages together along the left-hand side.

After Reading Encourage children to respond to what they've read by asking them what they liked most and least about the story. To assess their reading comprehension, ask children to do an oral retelling of the story.

Next, ask them to reflect on their experience reading the book. Where did they encounter problems and what did they do to solve them? Review parts of the text that children found challenging. Remind children to apply their knowledge of sound-spelling relationships when they get stuck on unfamiliar words. Also encourage them to use context clues in the text and pictures to figure out meanings.

You might also use this time to teach a mini-lesson on a particular phonics skill or to model good reading behaviors. For example, to demonstrate how punctuation affects your inflection, read aloud part of the text using somewhat exaggerated expression. Repeat the demonstration and then ask children to read aloud with you. If children have difficulty reading dialogue, demonstrate how to make the voices of each character distinct. Again, after you have read a sentence with expression, invite children to echo your reading.

You can help children build reading confidence by having them read each book several times. For more practice, children can pair up to read a book together and help each other with unfamiliar words. Again, tap into each child's progress by listening to individuals read aloud and by keeping notes.

Extending the Books

Connections to the Language Arts Standards

The activities in this book are designed to support you in meeting the following reading standards outlined by the Mid-continent Research for Education and Learning (McRel), an organization that collects and synthesizes national and state K–12 curriculum standards.

✻ Understands that print conveys meaning

✻ Understands how print is organized and read (e.g., identifies front and back covers, title pages, author, follows words from left-to-right and from top-to-bottom; knows the significance of spaces between words, knows the difference between letters, words, and sentences; understands the use of capitalization and punctuation as text boundaries)

✻ Creates mental images from pictures and print

✻ Uses basic elements of phonetic analysis to decode unknown words

✻ Understands level-appropriate sight words and vocabulary

✻ Uses self-correction strategies

✻ Reads aloud familiar stories with fluency and expression

Source—*Content Knowledge: A Compendium of Standards and Benchmarks for K–12 Education* (3rd ed.). (Mid-Continent Research for Education and Learning, 2000)

Little Reader Library Totes

Invite children to create their very own library totes for storing and carrying their little readers. Gather boxes sized about 6 to 7 inches wide, 4½ to 5 inches tall, and 2 to 3 inches deep. (Boxes containing packets of hot cereal or snack bars work well.) Then help children follow these steps to make their totes:

1. Securely tape any open flaps closed.

2. Use a glue stick to cover the outside of the box with gift wrap or craft paper.

3. Turn the box upside down. To make a hinged lid, make three cuts in the bottom of the box (now the top), as shown. (You can leave the side flaps on or cut them off.)

4. For a handle, staple a 12-inch piece of ribbon to the sides of the box, on the interior.

5. To make a closure, hot glue (adult only) a button or decorative bead to the front of the box, in the middle, as shown. Then affix a loop of ribbon or yarn to the underside of the lid, in the middle.

Children can decorate their totes using markers, stickers, and other craft materials.

Write a Little Reader

Using the language structure of different mini-books in the collection, children can try their hand at writing their very own books. For example, after children have read "What Is Red?" they might enjoy writing stories about other colors. On the chalkboard or chart paper, write another color word, such as *green*. Ask children to name things that are green. (*leaves, frogs, peas, grasshoppers,* and so on) Then write the sentence frame, _____ *are green. Green, green, green.* Provide children with white copy paper cut to quarter- or half-page size. On each page, have children copy and complete the sentence frame and draw a picture to illustrate it. Then have them write *What Is Green?* on a construction paper cover and staple the pages of their book together. Invite children to innovate on the text in other stories, as well, such as "What Do I Need?," "Almost Spring," and "Look What I Found!"

Sort and Read

To strengthen skills in critical thinking, reading comprehension, and interpreting context clues, have children practice sequencing the pages of some of the stories. Examples to try include "Hurry Up! Hurry Up!," "What Do I Need?," "Sweet Treat," "Cold Rose," and "I Can Draw!" Before photocopying, mask the numbers on the mini-book pages. Then make single-sided copies, cut apart the mini-book pages, and give them to children, out of order. Ask children to put the pages of the book in order and then read the book to a friend. Encourage them to talk with each other about why certain pages come before and after others, and why, in some books, more than one sequence of the pages might be reasonable. After this discussion, children can make any needed adjustments, number the pages, and staple their book together.

Reading and Writing Activities Across the Curriculum

Following are additional ideas and activities for extending the themes covered in this collection. Each activity is based on a book from one of the five main themes.

SCHOOL DAYS

Playground Opposites Wheel (Reading and Writing)

The story "Fun at the Playground" (pages 23–24) gives children practice reading high-frequency sight words that are opposites. To reinforce the pairs of opposites in the story, have children make Playground Opposites Wheels.

1. Give each child copies of pages 9–10. Invite children to color the wheels and then cut them out. (For added durability, have them glue the pages to oaktag before cutting.)

2. Show children how to cut out the window and flap door along the dotted lines.

3. Model how to place the shape wheel on top of the word/picture wheel, align the center dots, push a brass fastener through the dots, and open to secure.

4. To use their wheel, children turn the bottom wheel so the words appear in the window. Encourage them to read each word before lifting the flap to see the picture.

FRIENDS, FRIENDS, FRIENDS

Make a Sweet Treat! (Art and Writing)

Invite children to make their own ice-cream sundaes after reading the story "Sweet Treat" (pages 33–34). To start, give each child a copy of page 11, a sheet of construction paper, crayons, scissors, and a glue stick. Have children color the pictures and cut them out. Encourage them to use their imagination to create different flavors of ice cream. Then, using the construction paper as a background, have them assemble the ice-cream sundae of their dreams! (Have extra copies of the pattern page on hand for adding extra scoops.) Afterward, encourage children to label the parts of their sundae using the words in their "Sweet Treat" book (along with your help) as a reference tool. Then invite children to take turns describing the delicious-looking sundaes they created.

WHAT'S IN MY WORLD?

What Can I See? Magnifier Books (Science and Writing)

After reading "What Can I See?" (pages 43–44), invite children to make pretend magnifiers to get a close-up look at the world outdoors.

1. Give each child a copy of page 12. Have children glue the page to oaktag, cut out the magnifier pattern along the outer and inner dotted lines, and color.

2. Take children outdoors to a local park to make observations and take notes. Give children clipboards, paper, and pencils so they can record their findings. (For easy-to-make clipboards, give each child a binder clip and a piece of cardboard.) Encourage children to hold their magnifiers to their eyes for a focused look at their surroundings.

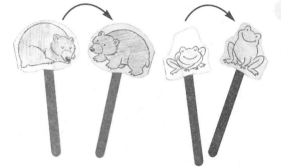

3. Back in the classroom, provide children with extra copies of the magnifier page. Instead of cutting out the center of the magnifier, children can use this space to record some of the things they observed on their walk using the sentence frame "I see _____." They can also draw pictures of the things they saw.

4. Afterward, have children add a magnifier cover with the title "What Can [child's name] See?" To bind their book, have children stack the pages, punch a hole in the handles, and use a brass fastener to secure them. To read their book, children can fan out the magnifier pages, one by one.

AROUND THE SEASONS

Hibernating Puppet Pals (Reading and Drama)

For a Reader's Theater version of "Winter Is Here" (pages 47–48), invite children to make puppets to dramatize the story during a rereading. Divide the class into groups of six and have each child choose the part of one of the animals. Give each group a copy of page 13 and have children color and cut out the two-sided animal patterns. Then direct them to fold the puppets in half and glue to a craft stick, as shown. As they read their page, have children show their animal going to sleep. When the group reaches the end of the story, tell children to gently "wake up" their animals as they read the last page together.

ALL ABOUT ME

I Can Draw a Clown! (Art and Writing)

After reading "I Can Draw!" (pages 55–56), give children a copy of page 14 and invite them to read and follow the illustrated directions to draw a clown just like the one in the story! Afterward, children can try writing their own set of directions for drawing other pictures and then exchange them with classmates.

Playground Opposites Wheel

top/arriba

La rueda de los opuestos

Playground Opposites Wheel

down abajo

in adentro

out afuera

up arriba

low bajo

high alto

bottom/abajo

La rueda de los opuestos

My First Bilingual Little Readers Scholastic Teaching Resources

Make a Sweet Treat!

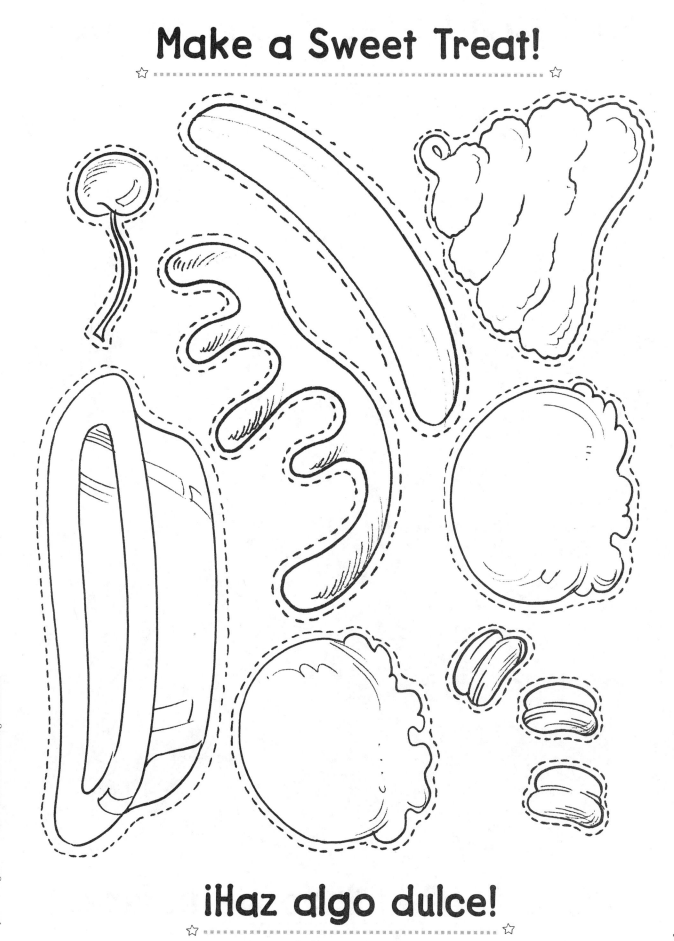

¡Haz algo dulce!

What Can I See? Magnifier Book

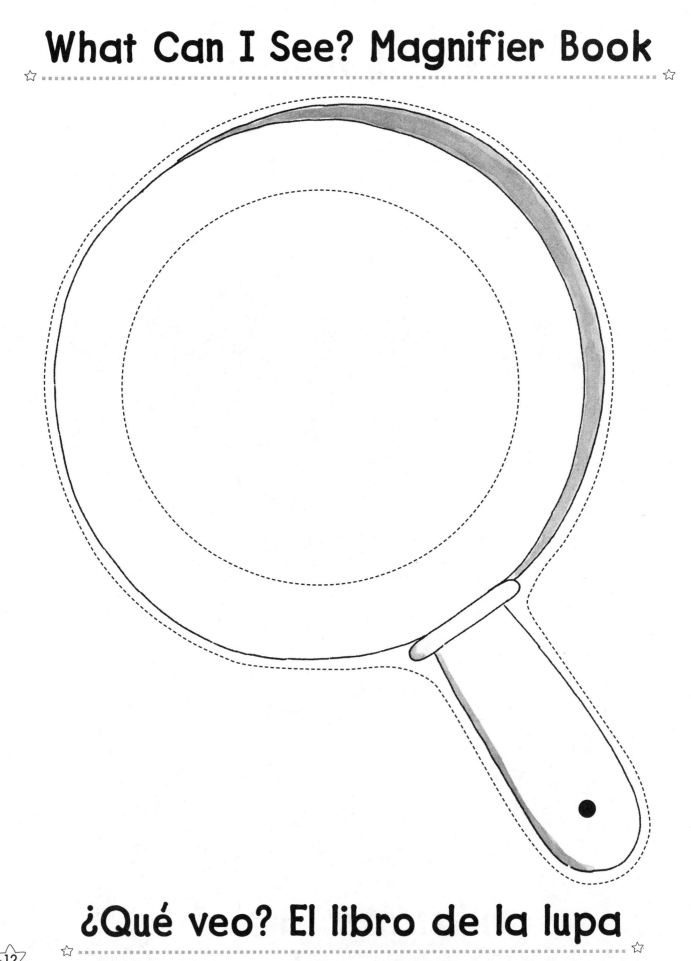

¿Qué veo? El libro de la lupa

Hibernating Puppet Pals

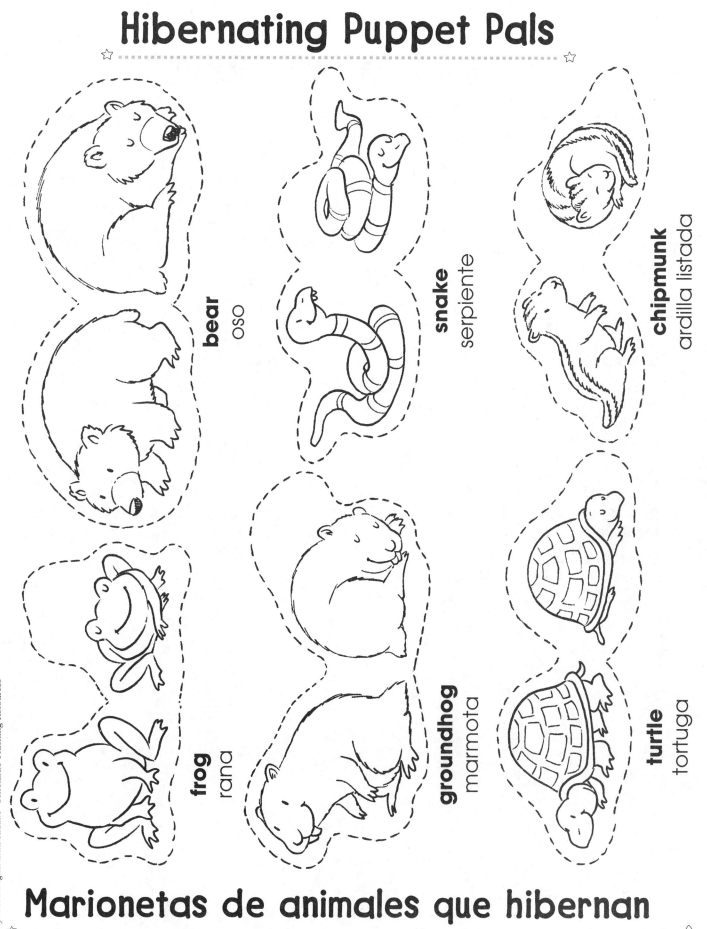

bear
oso

snake
serpiente

chipmunk
ardilla listada

frog
rana

groundhog
marmota

turtle
tortuga

Marionetas de animales que hibernan

I Can Draw a Clown!

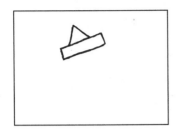

1. Draw a rectangle and a triangle for the hat.

Dibuja un rectángulo y un triángulo para el sombrero.

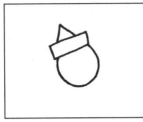

2. Draw an oval for the head.

Dibuja un óvalo para la cabeza.

3. Draw a curved rectangle for the collar.

Dibuja un rectángulo curvo para el cuello de la camisa.

4. Draw 2 rectangles for arms.

Dibuja 2 rectángulos para los brazos.

5. Draw 2 lines for the shirt.

Dibuja 2 líneas para la camisa.

6. Draw 2 hands.

Dibuja las 2 manos.

7. Draw hair and a face.

Dibuja el pelo y la cara.

8. Draw 2 buttons!

¡Dibuja dos botones!

Puedo dibujar un payaso!

Hurry Up! Hurry Up! Hurry Up!
¡De prisa! ¡De prisa!

Get dressed.
Hurry up! Hurry up!

Vístete.
¡De prisa! ¡De prisa!

My First Bilingual Little Readers Scholastic Teaching Resources

Eat breakfast.
Hurry up! Hurry up!

Desayuna.
¡De prisa! ¡De prisa!

It is the first day of school!
Hurry up! Hurry up!

¡Es el primer día de escuela!
¡De prisa! ¡De prisa!

1

Get out of bed.
Hurry up! Hurry up!

Levántate de la cama.
¡De prisa! ¡De prisa!

2

Brush my teeth.
Hurry up! Hurry up!

Cepíllate los dientes.
¡De prisa! ¡De prisa!

6

Get the bus.
Hurry up! Hurry up!

Toma el autobús.
¡De prisa! ¡De prisa!

5

Take my lunch.
Hurry up! Hurry up!

Lleva el almuerzo.
¡De prisa! ¡De prisa!

Me gusta recortar.

I like to cut.

I Like School!

¡Me gusta la escuela!

Me gusta pegar.

I like to glue.

En un barco puedo navegar. El barco es grande y rojo.

I like school!

¡Me gusta la escuela!

Me gusta leer.

I like to read.

Me gusta pintar.

I like to paint.

I like to write.

Me gusta escribir.

Me gusta contar.

I like to count.

The mouse crawls
around and around.

El ratón se desliza
por todas partes.

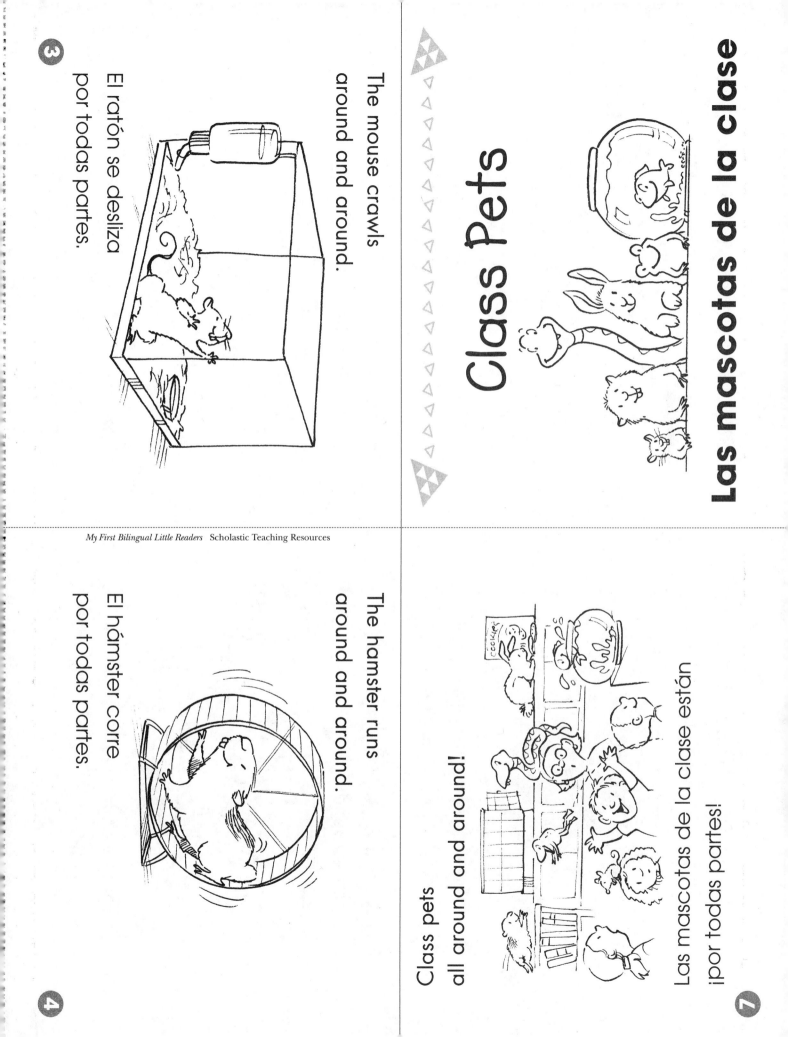

Class Pets

Las mascotas de la clase

My First Bilingual Little Readers Scholastic Teaching Resources

The hamster runs
around and around.

El hámster corre
por todas partes.

Class pets
all around and around!

Las mascotas de la clase
¡por todas partes!

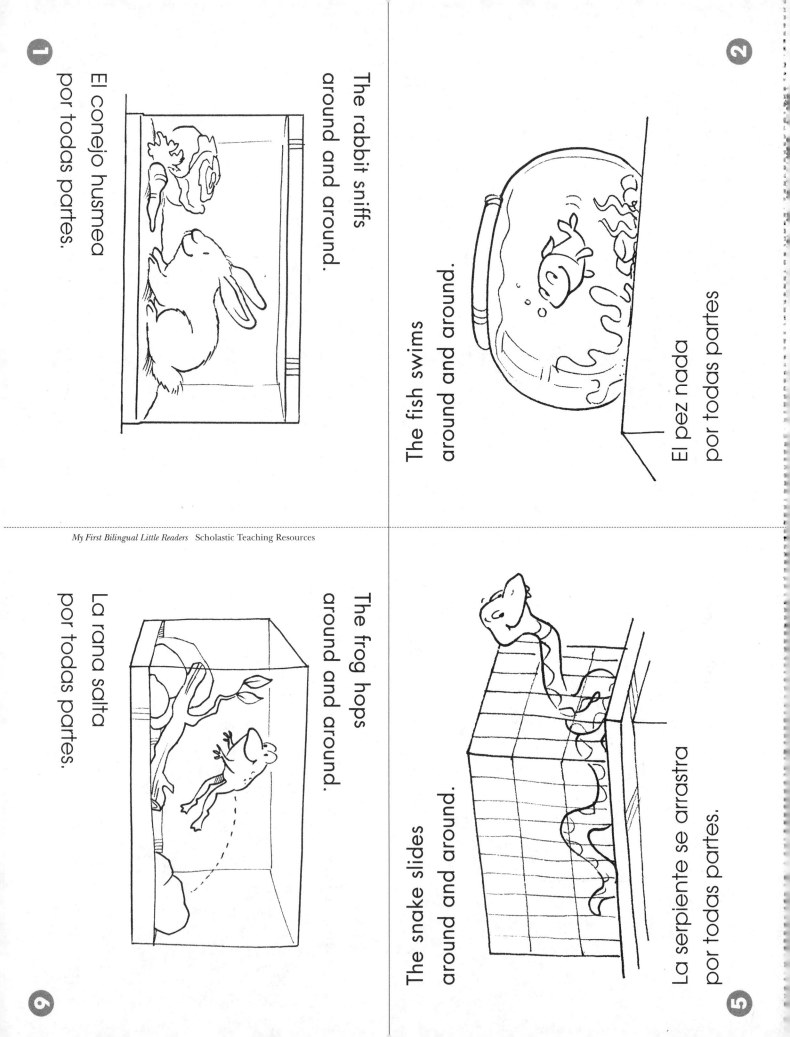

The fish swims
around and around.

El pez nada
por todas partes

The rabbit sniffs
around and around.

El conejo husmea
por todas partes.

My First Bilingual Little Readers   Scholastic Teaching Resources

The snake slides
around and around.

La serpiente se arrastra
por todas partes.

The frog hops
around and around.

La rana salta
por todas partes.

Shapes for Lunch

Figuras para el almuerzo

I like to eat ovals.

Me gusta comer óvalos.

3

I like to eat rectangles.

Me gusta comer rectángulos.

4

Shapes are fun
for lunch!

¡Comer figuras
es muy divertido!

7

Me gusta comer triángulos.

I like to eat triangles.

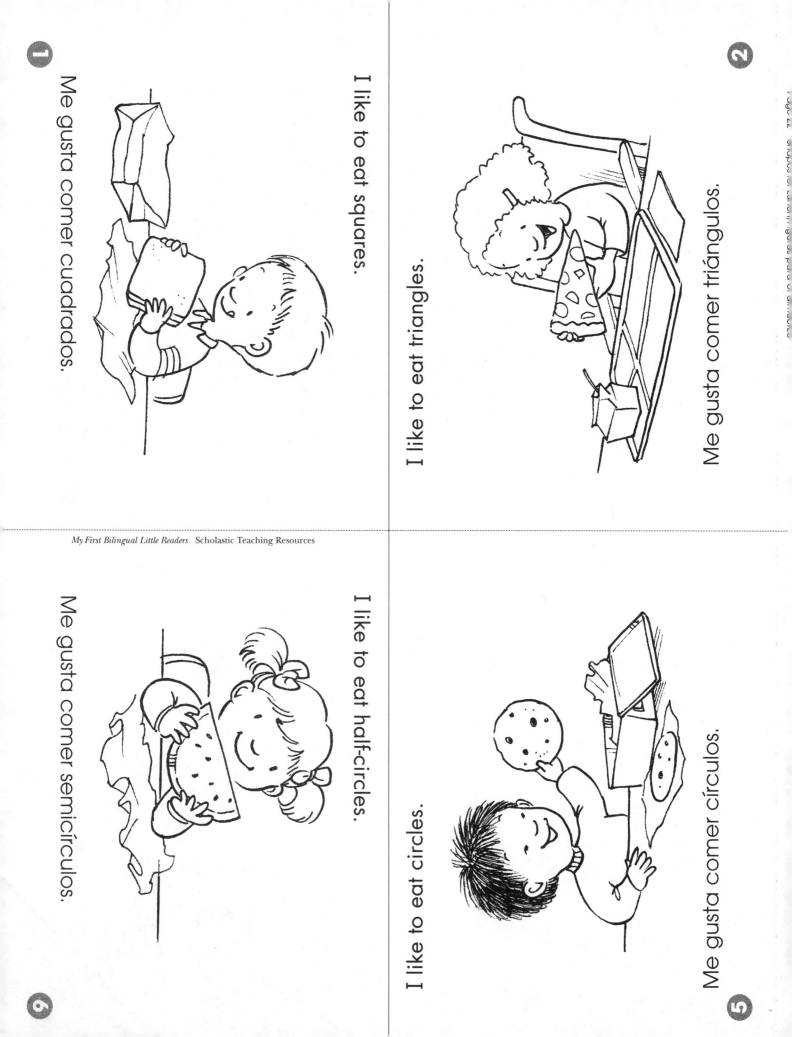

I like to eat squares.

Me gusta comer cuadrados.

Me gusta comer círculos.

I like to eat circles.

I like to eat half-circles.

Me gusta comer semicírculos.

Voy hasta arriba.

I go high.

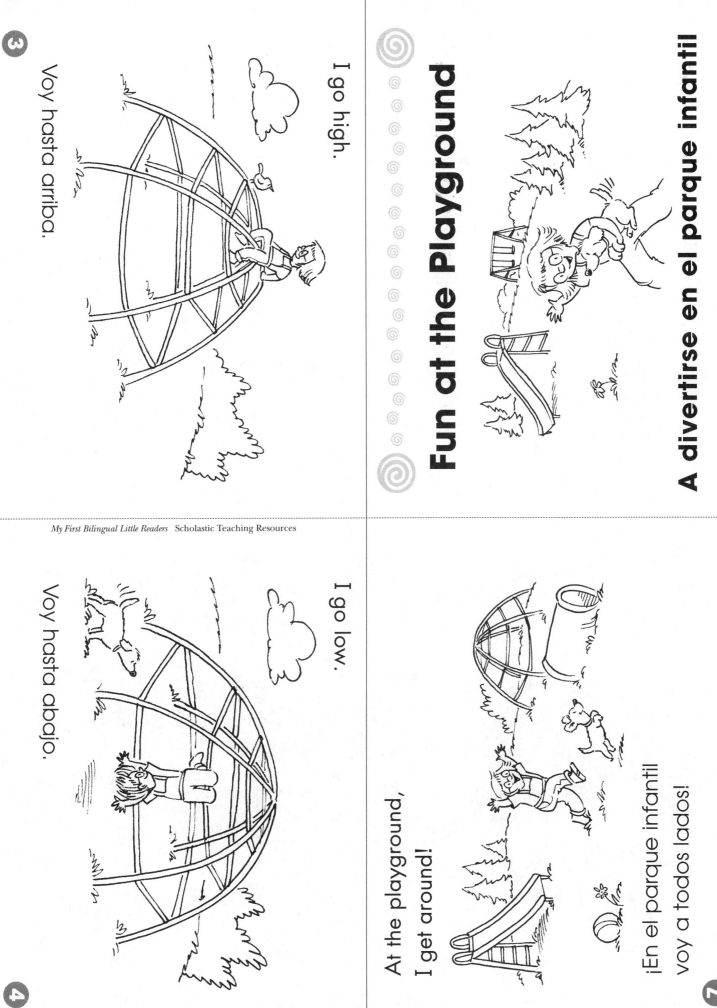

Fun at the Playground

A divertirse en el parque infantil

Voy hasta abajo.

I go low.

At the playground,
I get around!

¡En el parque infantil
voy a todos lados!

I go in.

Entro.

I go out.

Salgo.

I go down.

Bajo.

I go up.

Subo.

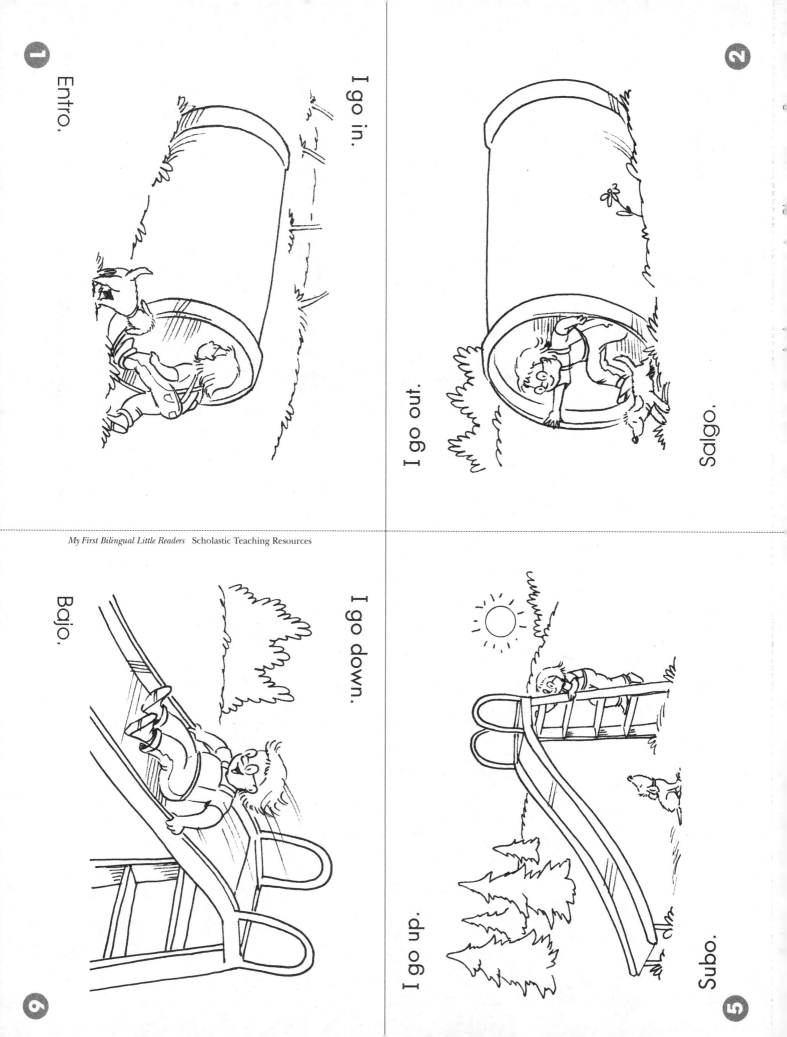

I need a blanket.

Necesito una manta.

What Do I Need?

¿Qué necesito?

I need a pillow.

Necesito una almohada.

I need a friend!

¡Necesito una amiga!

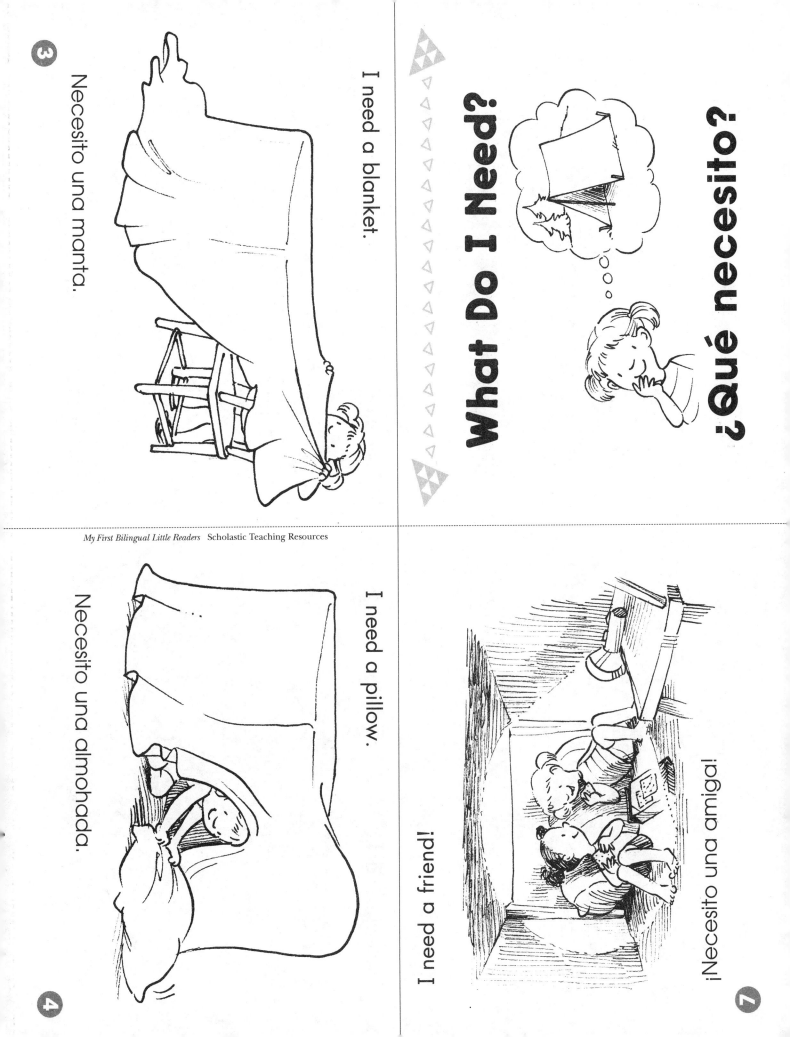

1

I need a table.

Necesito una mesa.

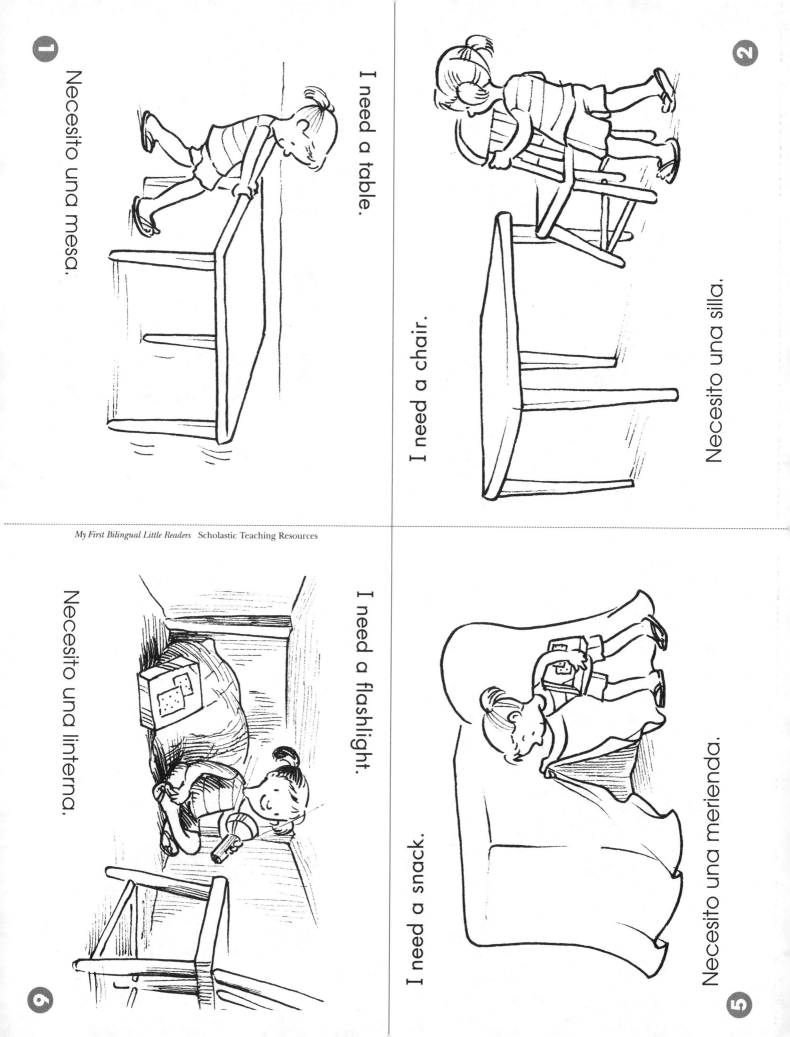

2

I need a chair.

Necesito una silla.

6

I need a flashlight.

Necesito una linterna.

5

I need a snack.

Necesito una merienda.

I have ribbon.

Tengo cinta.

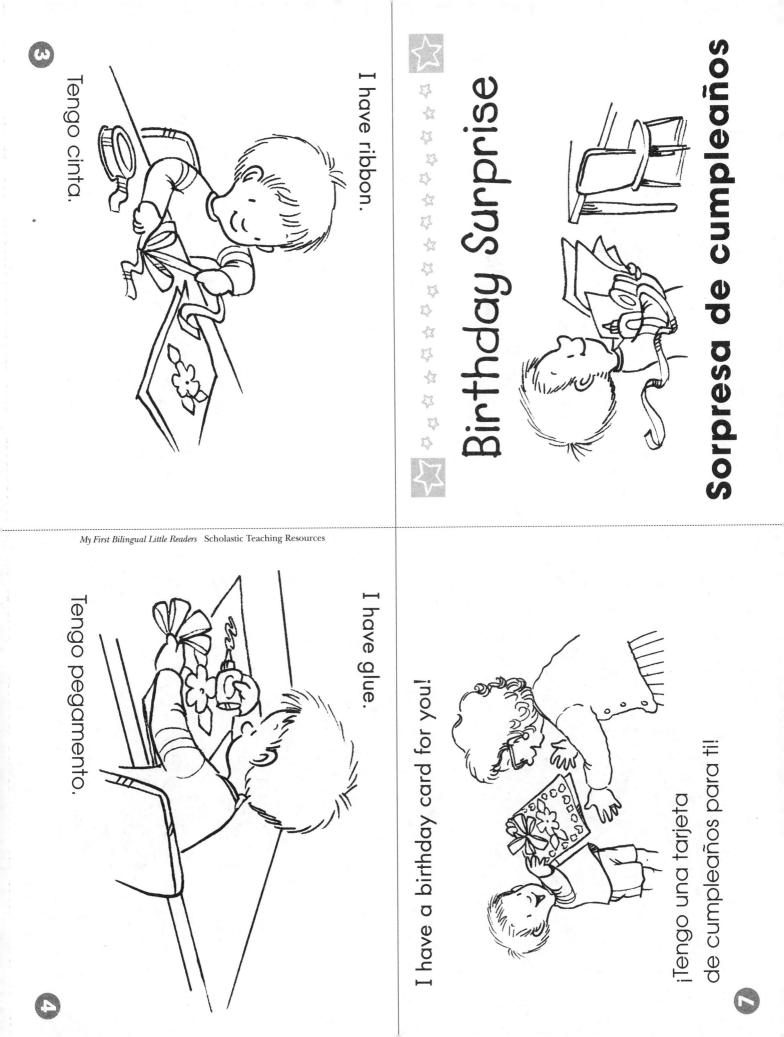

sorpresa de cumpleaños

My First Bilingual Little Readers   Scholastic Teaching Resources

I have glue.

Tengo pegamento.

I have a birthday card for you!

¡Tengo una tarjeta
de cumpleaños para ti!

Tengo papel.

I have paper.

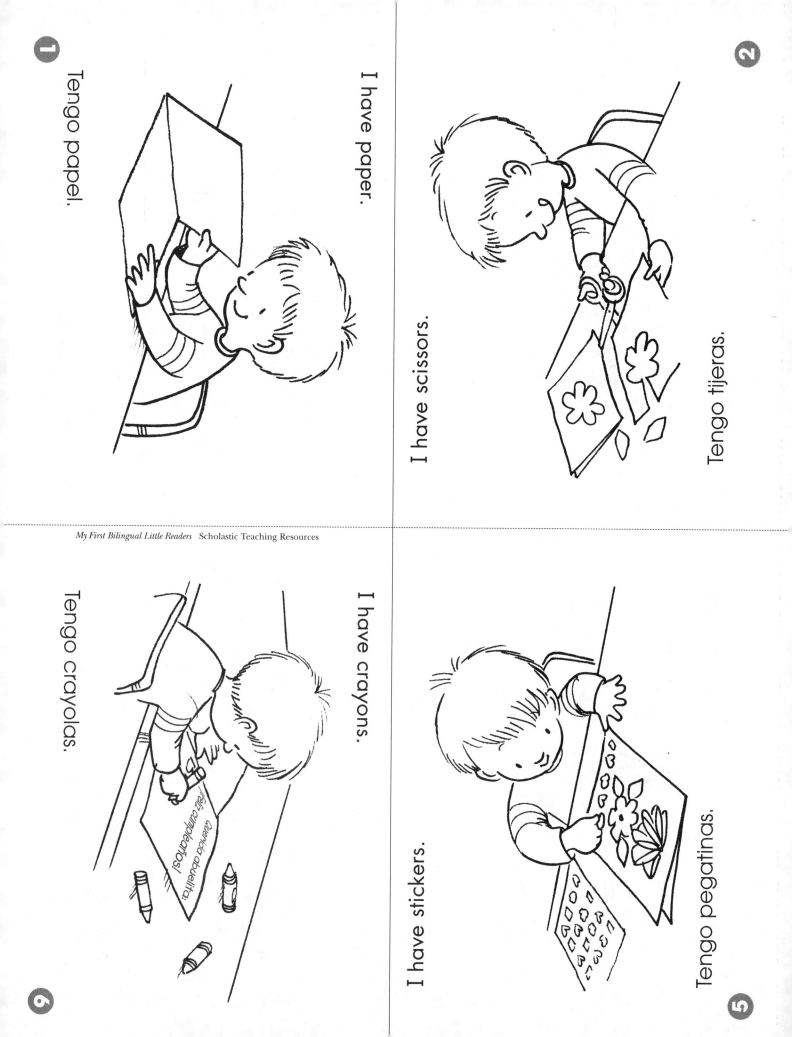

Tengo tijeras.

I have scissors.

Tengo crayolas.

I have crayons.

¡Querida abuelita! ¡Feliz cumpleaños!

Tengo pegatinas.

I have stickers.

Fun With Mud

A divertirse en el barro

Mud pies.

Tortas de barro.

3

Mud donuts.

Rosquillas de barro.

4

Bake sale!

¡Venta de pasteles!

7

Galletas de barro.

Mud cookies.

Pasteles de barro.

Mud cakes.

Pan de barro.

Mud bread.

Bizcochos de barro.

Mud muffins.

3

¿Está detrás de la puerta?

Is he behind the door?

Where Is Petey?

¿Dónde está Pedrito?

¿Está en la gaveta?

Is he in the drawer?

4

Here is Petey!

¡Aquí está Pedrito!

7

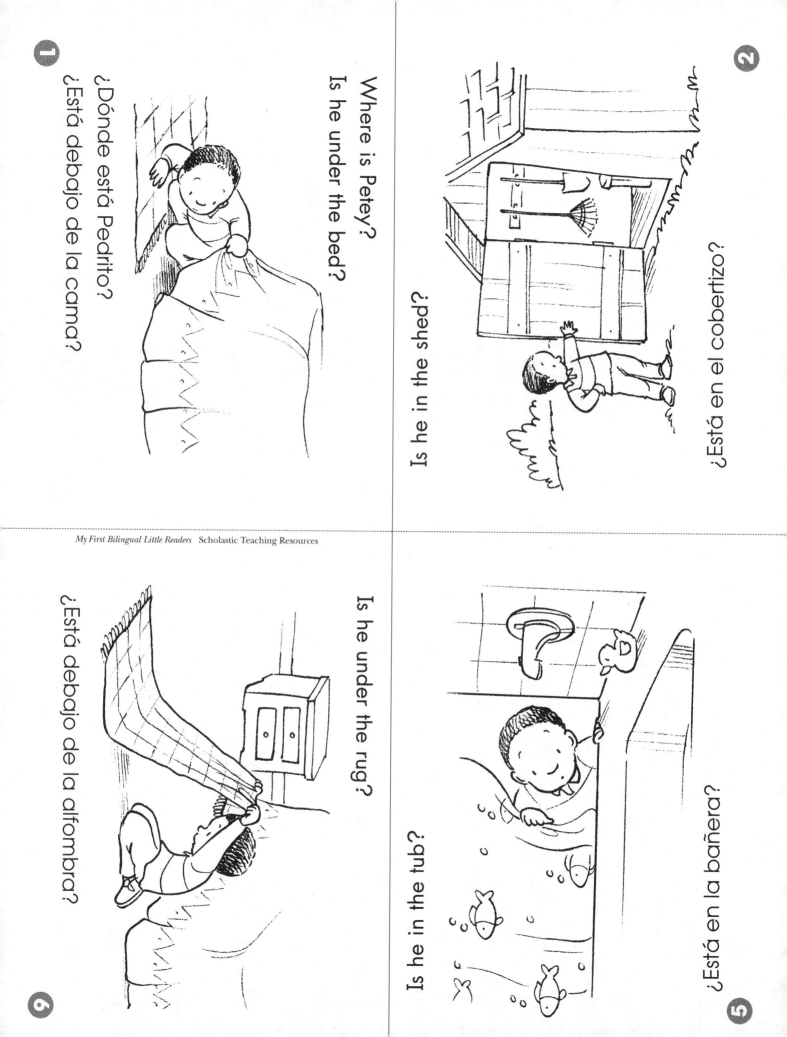

1

Where is Petey?
Is he under the bed?

¿Dónde está Pedrito?
¿Está debajo de la cama?

2

Is he in the shed?

¿Está en el cobertizo?

5

Is he in the tub?

¿Está en la bañera?

6

Is he under the rug?

¿Está debajo de la alfombra?

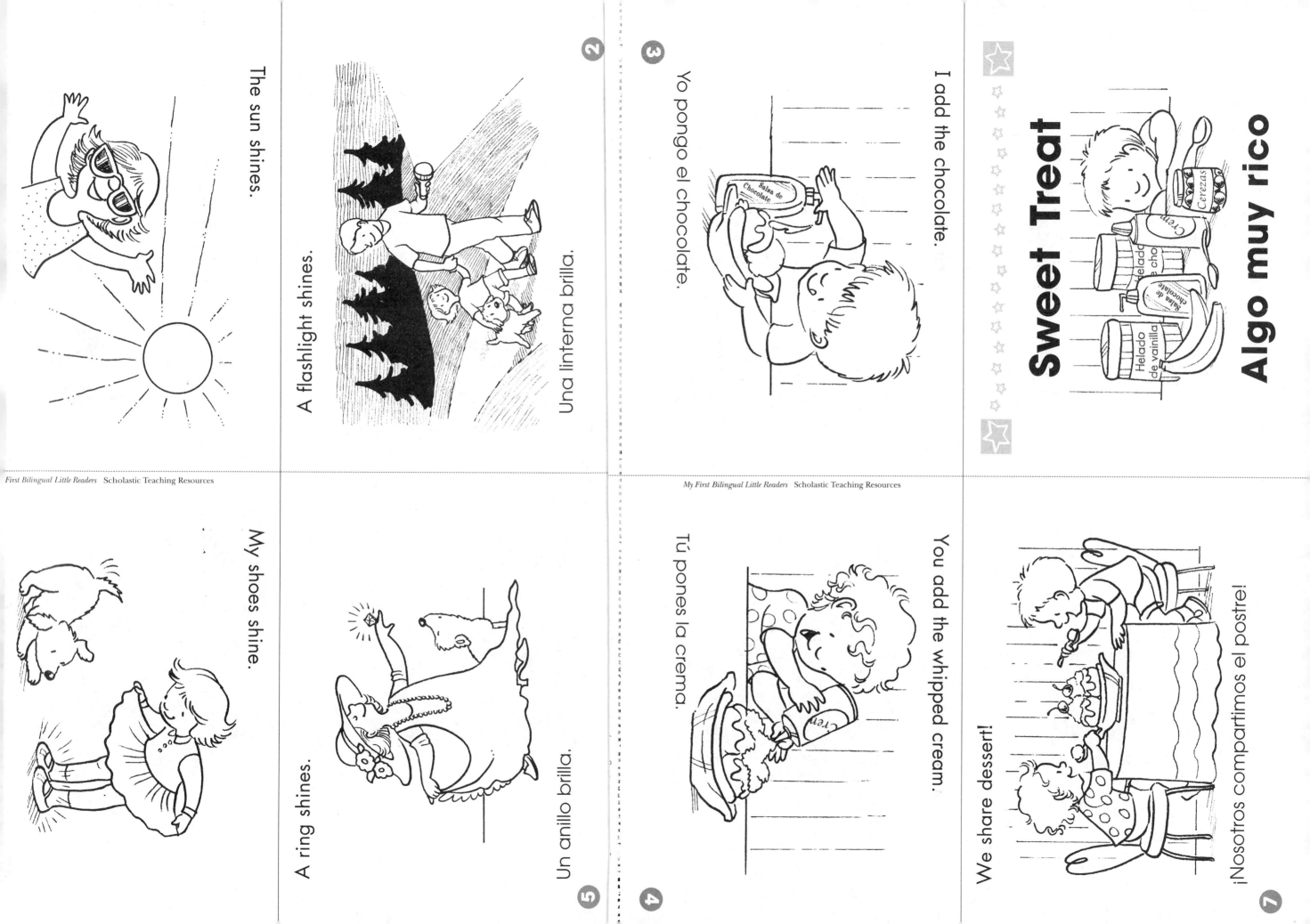

The sun shines.

② A flashlight shines.
Una linterna brilla.

③ I add the chocolate.
Yo pongo el chocolate.

⭐ **Sweet Treat**
Algo muy rico

My shoes shine.

⑤ A ring shines.
Un anillo brilla.

④ You add the whipped cream.
Tú pones la crema.

⑦ We share dessert!
¡Nosotros compartimos el postre!

① Yo pongo el plátano.

I add the banana.

② You add the ice cream.

Helado de cho[...]

Helado de vainilla

Tú pones el helado.

③ La luna brilla.

The moon shines.

What Shines?

① El sol brilla.

⑥ Tú pones las cerezas.

You add the cherries.

Cerezas

⑤ You add the cherries.

I add the nuts.

Yo pongo las nueces.

④ Una moneda brilla.

A coin shines.

⑥ Mis zapatos brillan.

I shine!

I Like Stripes

Me gustan las rayas

3

A flag has stripes.
I like stripes.

La bandera tiene rayas.
Me gustan las rayas.

4

A zebra has stripes.
I like stripes.

La zebra tiene rayas.
Me gustan las rayas.

7

A ladybug has spots.
I like spots!

La mariquita tiene lunares.
¡Me gustan los lunares!

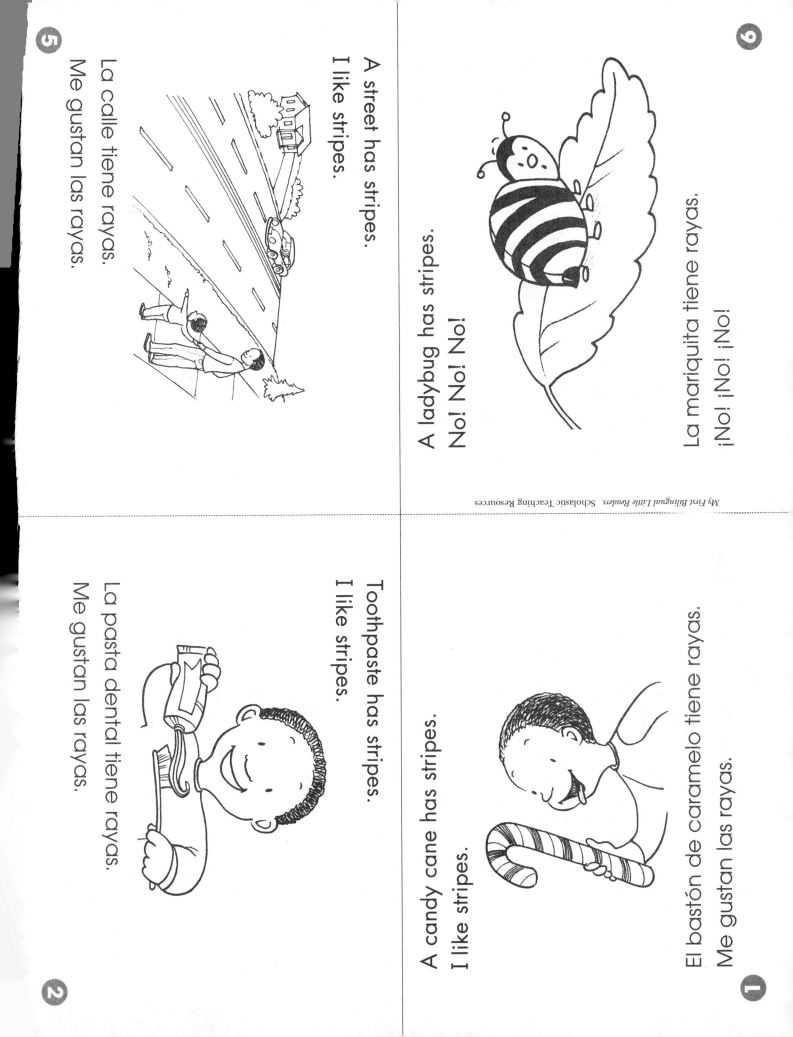

A ladybug has stripes.
No! No! No!

La mariquita tiene rayas.
¡No! ¡No! ¡No!

A street has stripes.
I like stripes.

La calle tiene rayas.
Me gustan las rayas.

Toothpaste has stripes.
I like stripes.

La pasta dental tiene rayas.
Me gustan las rayas.

A candy cane has stripes.
I like stripes.

El bastón de caramelo tiene rayas.
Me gustan las rayas.

My face is red.
Red, red, red!

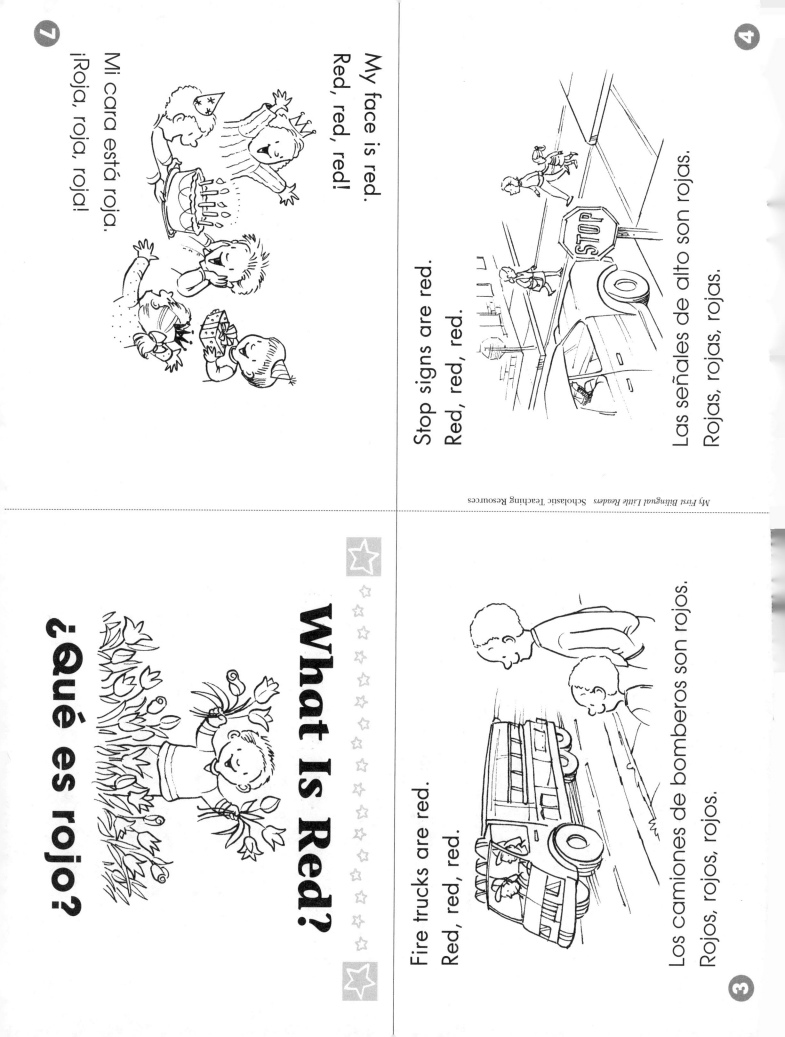

Mi cara está roja.
¡Roja, roja, roja!

Stop signs are red.
Red, red, red.

Las señales de alto son rojas.
Rojas, rojas, rojas.

What Is Red!

¿Qué es rojo?

Fire trucks are red.
Red, red, red.

Los camiones de bomberos son rojos.
Rojos, rojos, rojos.

Strawberries are red.
Red, red, red.

Las fresas son rojas.
Rojas, rojas, rojas.

Apples are red.
Red, red, red.

Las manzanas son rojas.
Rojas, rojas, rojas.

Flowers are red.
Red, red, red.

Las flores son rojas.
Rojas, rojas, rojas.

Hearts are red.
Red, red, red.

Los corazones son rojas.
Rojos, rojos, rojos.

Yo pongo el chocolate.

I add the chocolate.

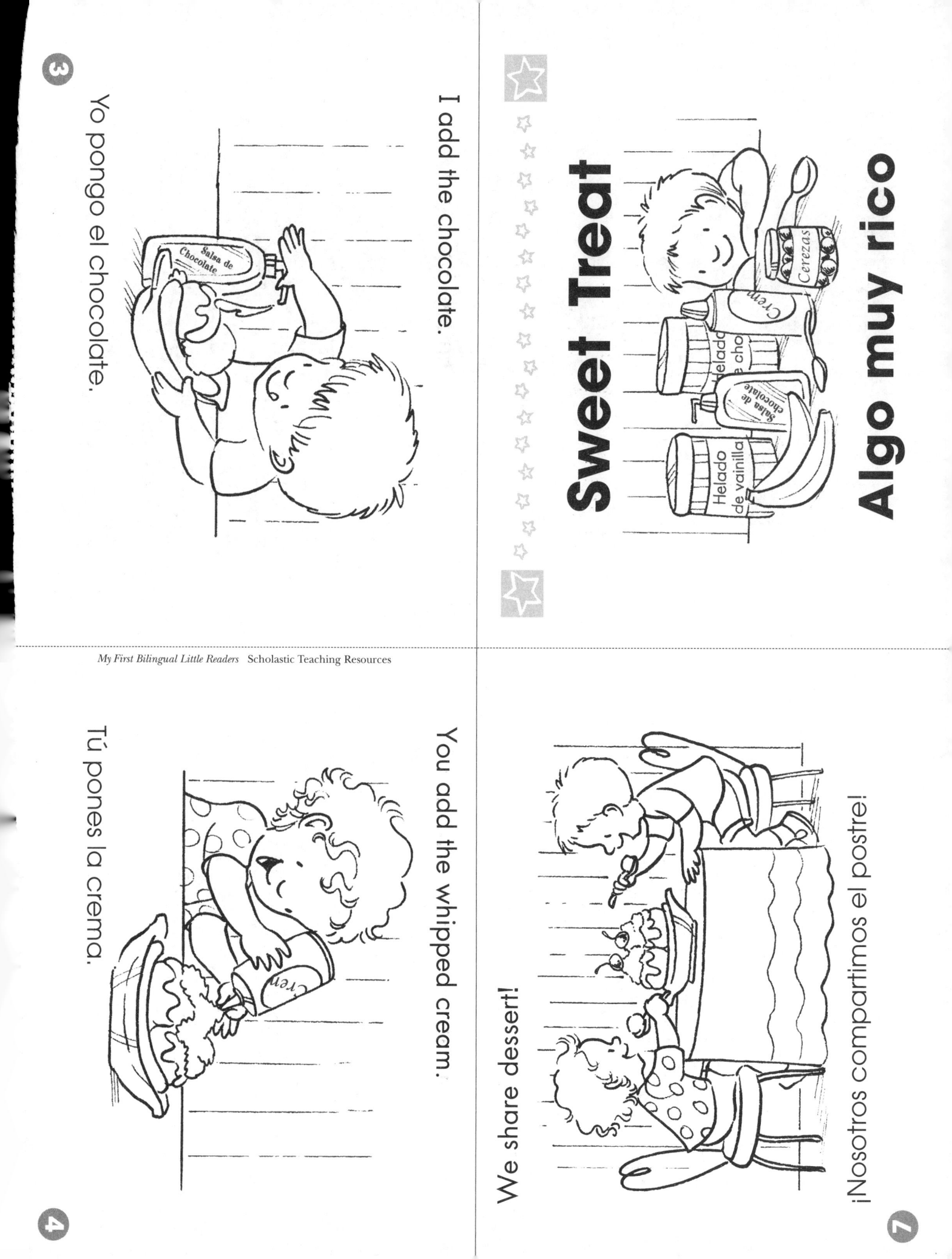

Sweet Treat

Algo muy rico

Tú pones la crema.

You add the whipped cream.

We share dessert!

¡Nosotros compartimos el postre!

You add the cherries.

Tú pones las cerezas.

Cerezas

I add the nuts.

Yo pongo las nueces.

My First Bilingual Little Readers Scholastic Teaching Resources

You add the ice cream.

Tú pones el helado.

Helado de vainilla

Helado de cho

I add the banana.

Yo pongo el plátano.

¡Yo brillo!

I shine!

A coin shines.

Una moneda brilla.

¿Qué brilla?

What Shines?

The moon shines.

La luna brilla.

Un anillo brilla.

A ring shines.

My shoes shine.

Mis zapatos brillan.

Una linterna brilla.

A flashlight shines.

The sun shines.

El sol brilla.

Bubbles!
¡Burbujas!

Bubbles in the sink.

Burbujas en el fregadero.

Bubbles in my drink.

Burbujas en mi bebida.

Bubbles, bubbles, bubbles, everywhere I go!

¡Burbujas, burbujas, por donde quiera que voy!

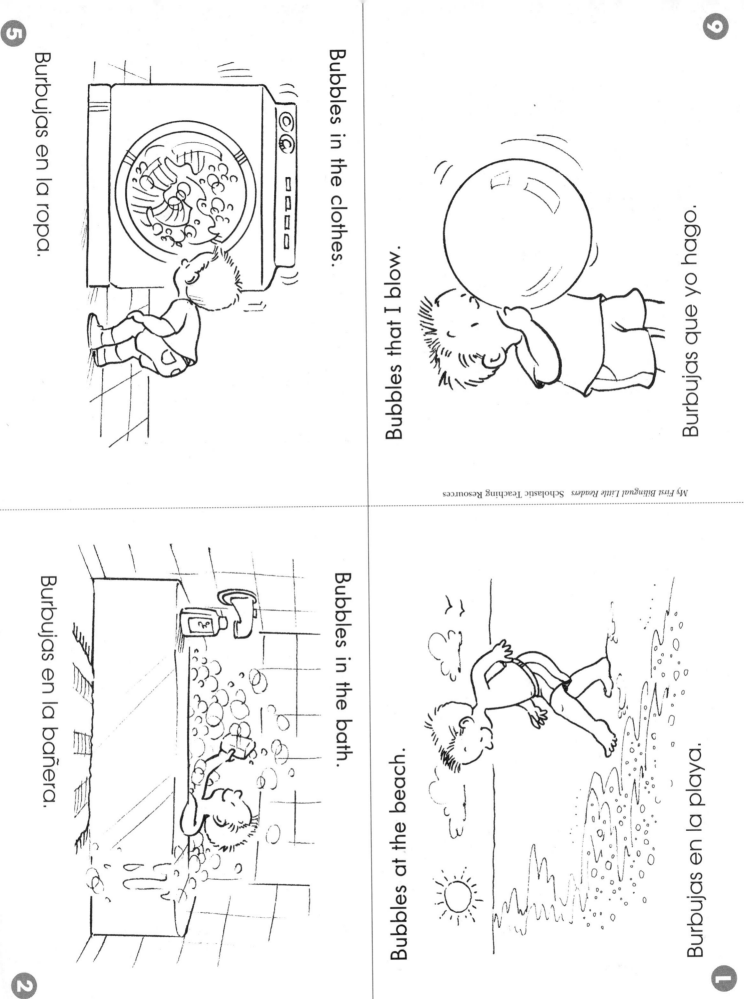

5

Bubbles in the clothes.

Burbujas en la ropa.

6

Bubbles that I blow.

Burbujas que yo hago.

My First Bilingual Little Readers Scholastic Teaching Resources

2

Bubbles in the bath.

Burbujas en la bañera.

1

Bubbles at the beach.

Burbujas en la playa.

But no one can see me!

¡Pero nadie me puede ver a mí!

I see a home.

Veo una casa.

What Can I See?

¿Qué veo?

I see a leaf.

Veo una hoja.

I see a bee.

Veo una abeja.

I see a flower.

Veo una flor.

My First Bilingual Little Readers   Scholastic Teaching Resources

I see a stone.

Veo una piedra.

I see an ant.

Veo una hormiga.

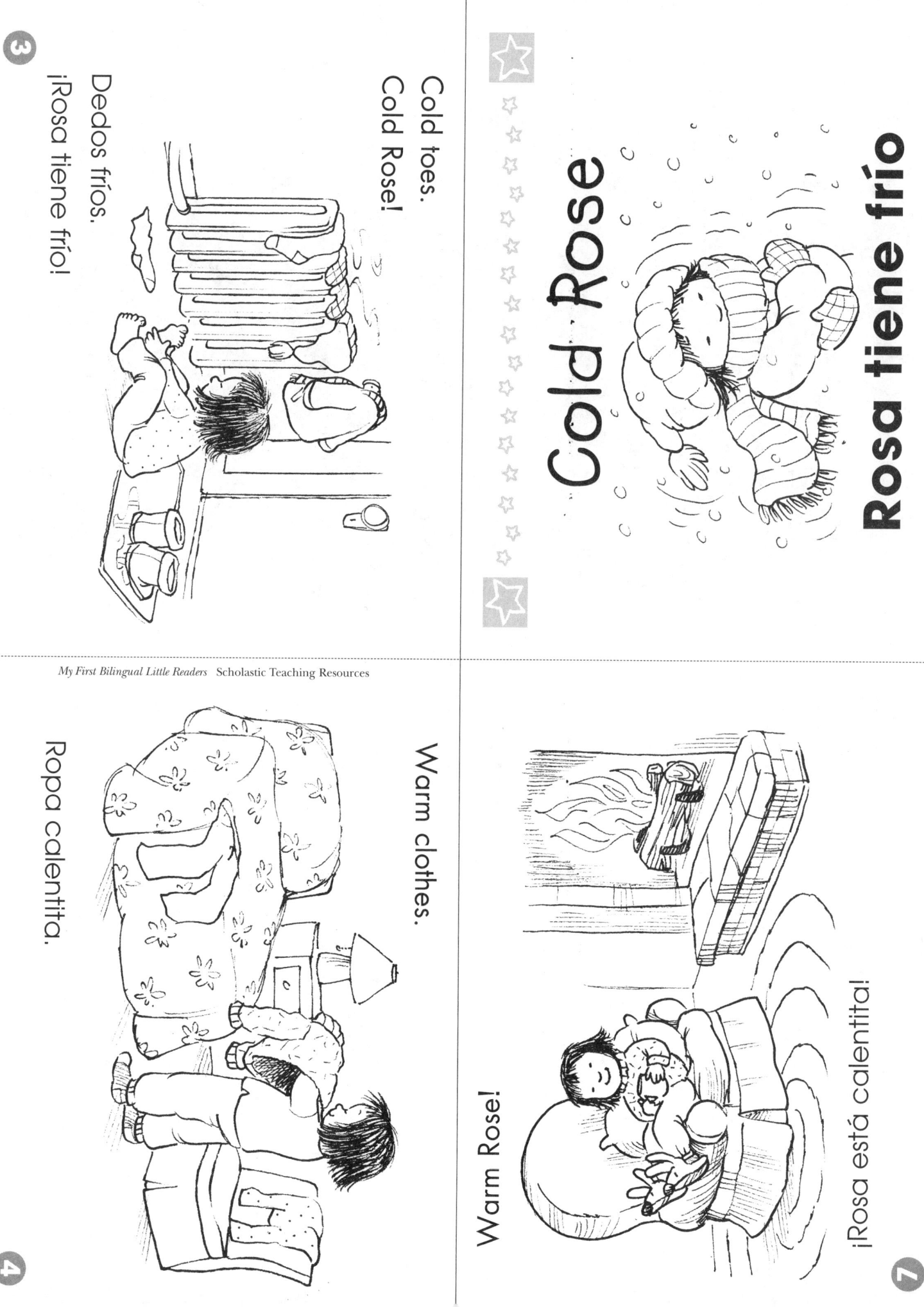

Cold Rose

Rosa tiene frío

Cold toes.
Cold Rose!

Dedos fríos.
¡Rosa tiene frío!

Warm clothes.

Ropa calentita.

Warm Rose!

¡Rosa está calentita!

3

4

7

Dedos calentitos.

Warm toes.

Nariz calentita.

Warm nose.

My First Bilingual Little Readers Scholastic Teaching Resources

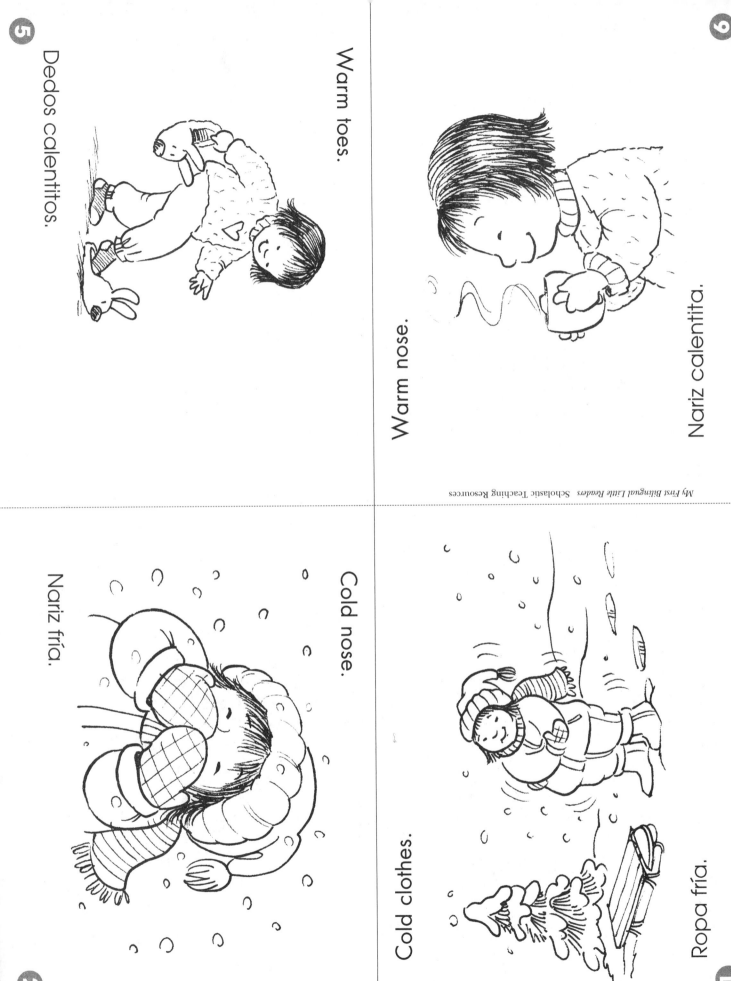

Nariz fría.

Cold nose.

Cold clothes.

Ropa fría.

Spring is here.
Time to wake up!

Llegó la primavera.
¡Ya es hora de despertar!

Winter is here.
Sleep, frog, sleep.

Llegó el invierno.
Duerme, rana, duerme.

My First Bilingual Little Readers Scholastic Teaching Resources

Winter Is Here

Llegó el invierno

Winter is here.
Sleep, chipmunk, sleep.

Llegó el invierno.
Duerme, ardilla listada, duerme.

Winter is here.
Sleep, groundhog, sleep.

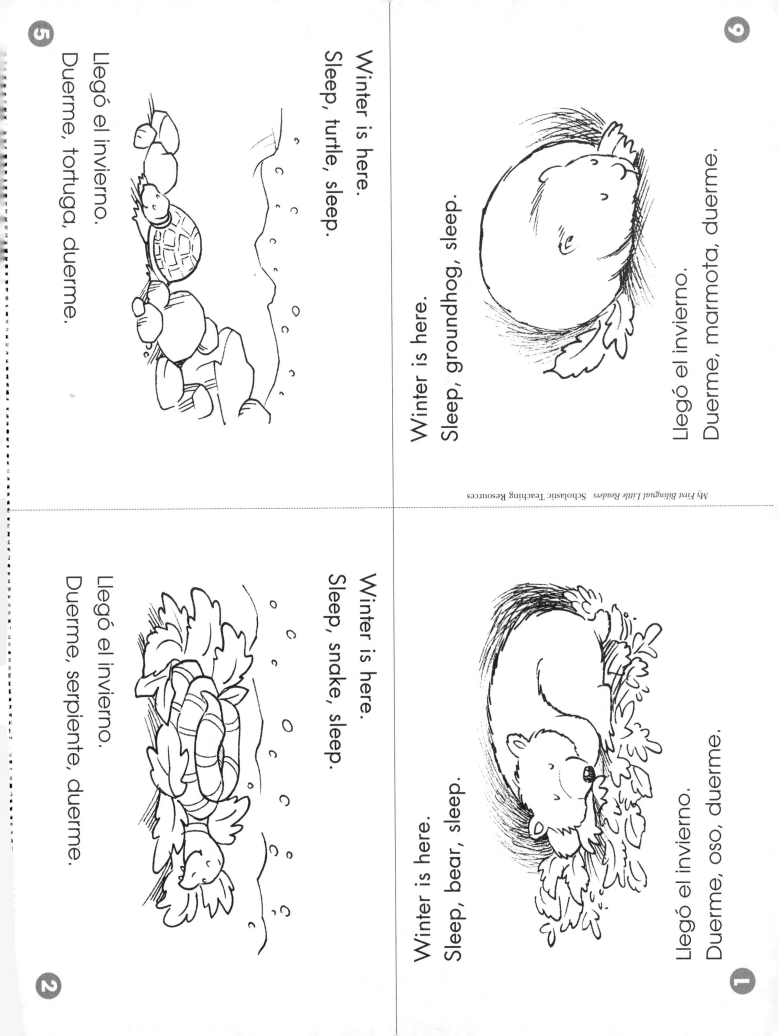

Llegó el invierno.
Duerme, marmota, duerme.

My First Bilingual Little Readers   Scholastic Teaching Resources

Winter is here.
Sleep, turtle, sleep.

Llegó el invierno.
Duerme, tortuga, duerme.

Winter is here.
Sleep, snake, sleep.

Llegó el invierno.
Duerme, serpiente, duerme.

Winter is here.
Sleep, bear, sleep.

Llegó el invierno.
Duerme, oso, duerme.

Birds are singing.
It is almost spring.

Los pájaros cantan.
Ya casi es primavera.

Almost Spring

Ya casi es primavera

My First Bilingual Little Readers Scholastic Teaching Resources

Flowers are budding.
It is almost spring.

Las flores comienzan a salir.
Ya casi es primavera.

Spring is here!

¡Ya llegó la primavera!

Wind is blowing.
It is almost spring.

El viento sopla.
Ya casi es primavera.

Chicks are peeping.
It is almost spring.

Los pollitos asoman la cabeza.
Ya casi es primavera.

Snow is melting.
It is almost spring.

La nieve se derrite.
Ya casi es primavera.

Sun is shining.
It is almost spring.

El sol brilla.
Ya casi es primavera.

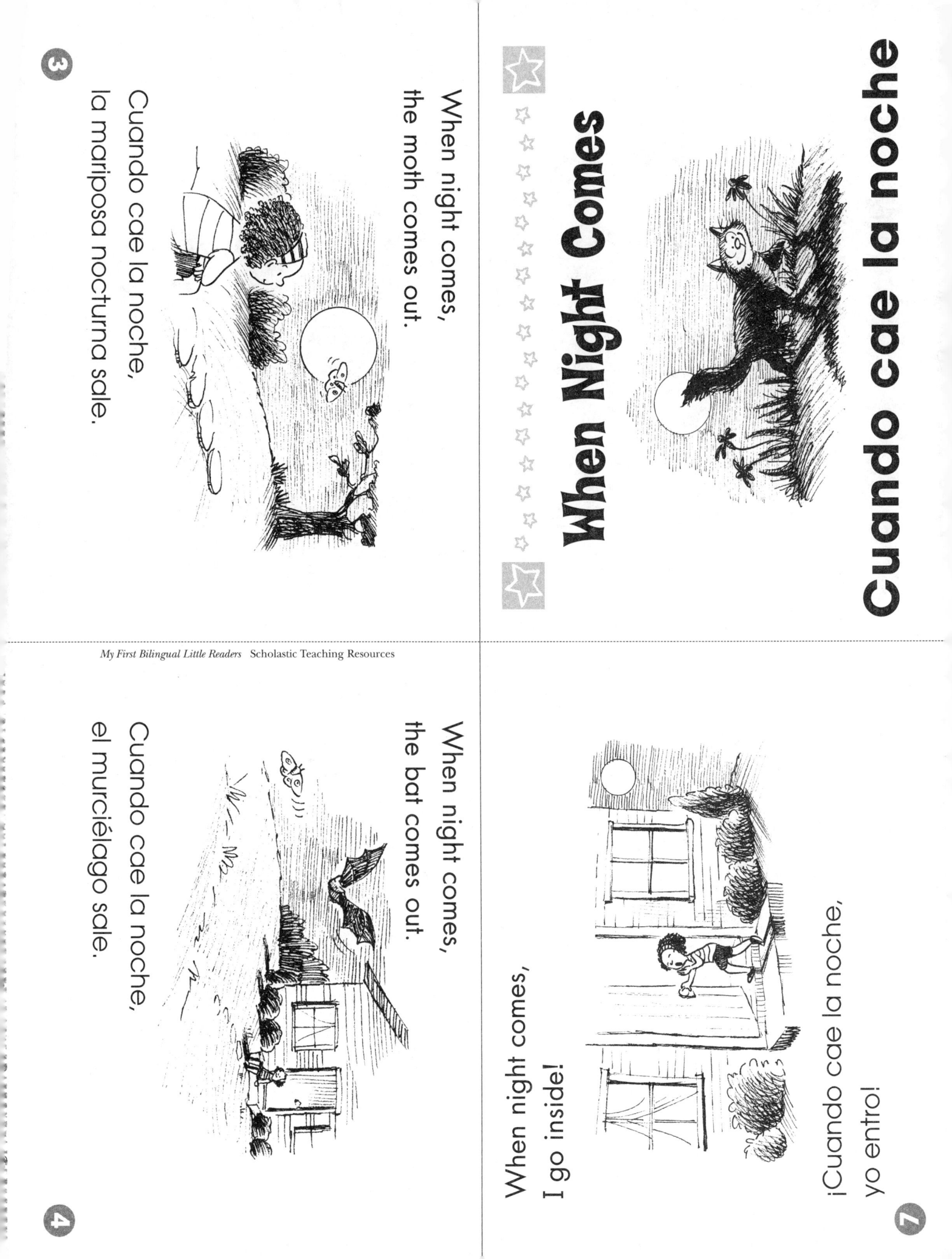

When Night Comes

Cuando cae la noche

When night comes,
the moth comes out.

Cuando cae la noche,
la mariposa nocturna sale.

3

When night comes,
the bat comes out.

Cuando cae la noche,
el murciélago sale.

4

When night comes,
I go inside!

¡Cuando cae la noche,
yo entro!

7

5

When night comes,
the firefly comes out.

Cuando cae la noche,
la luciérnaga sale.

6

When night comes,
the cat comes out.

Cuando cae la noche,
el gato sale.

2

When night comes,
the owl comes out.

Cuando cae la noche,
la lechuza sale.

1

When night comes,
the mouse comes out.

Cuando cae la noche,
el ratón sale.

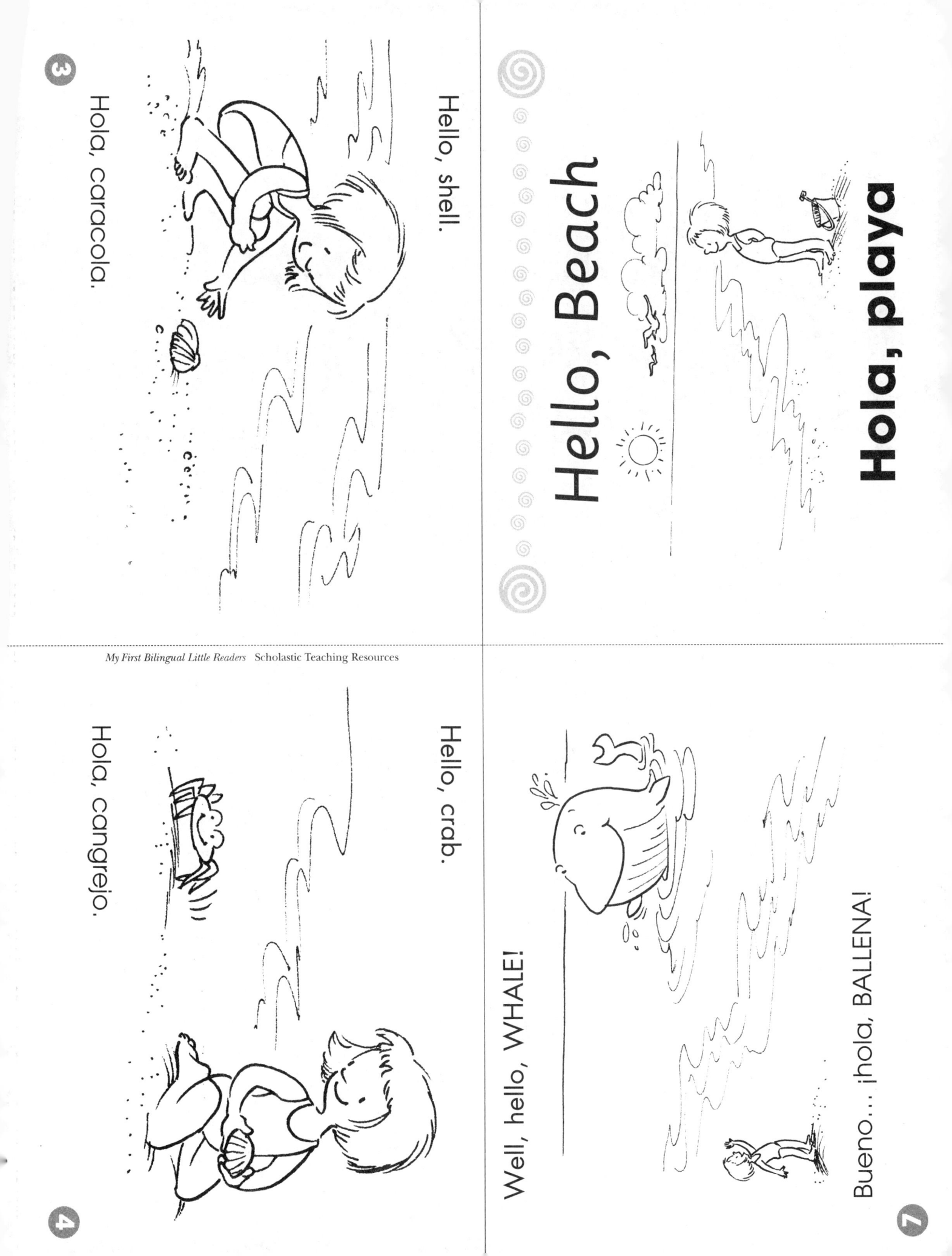

3

Hello, shell.

Hola, caracola.

Hola, playa

Hello, Beach

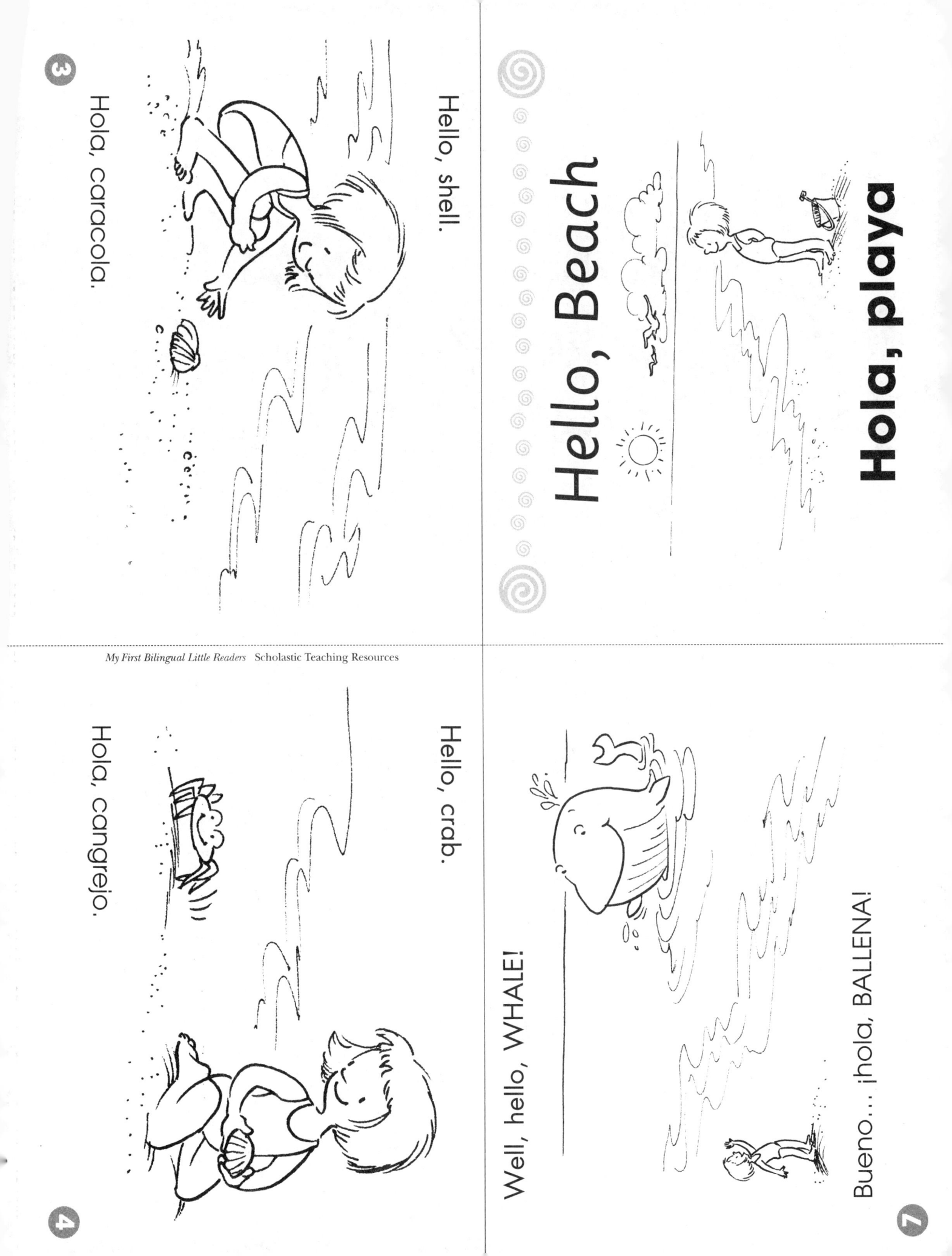

4

Hello, crab.

Hola, cangrejo.

Well, hello, WHALE!

Bueno... ¡hola, BALLENA!

7

Hello, sun.

Hola, sol.

Hello, sand.

Hola, arena.

Hello, sail.

Hola, velero.

Hello, gull.

Hola, gaviota.

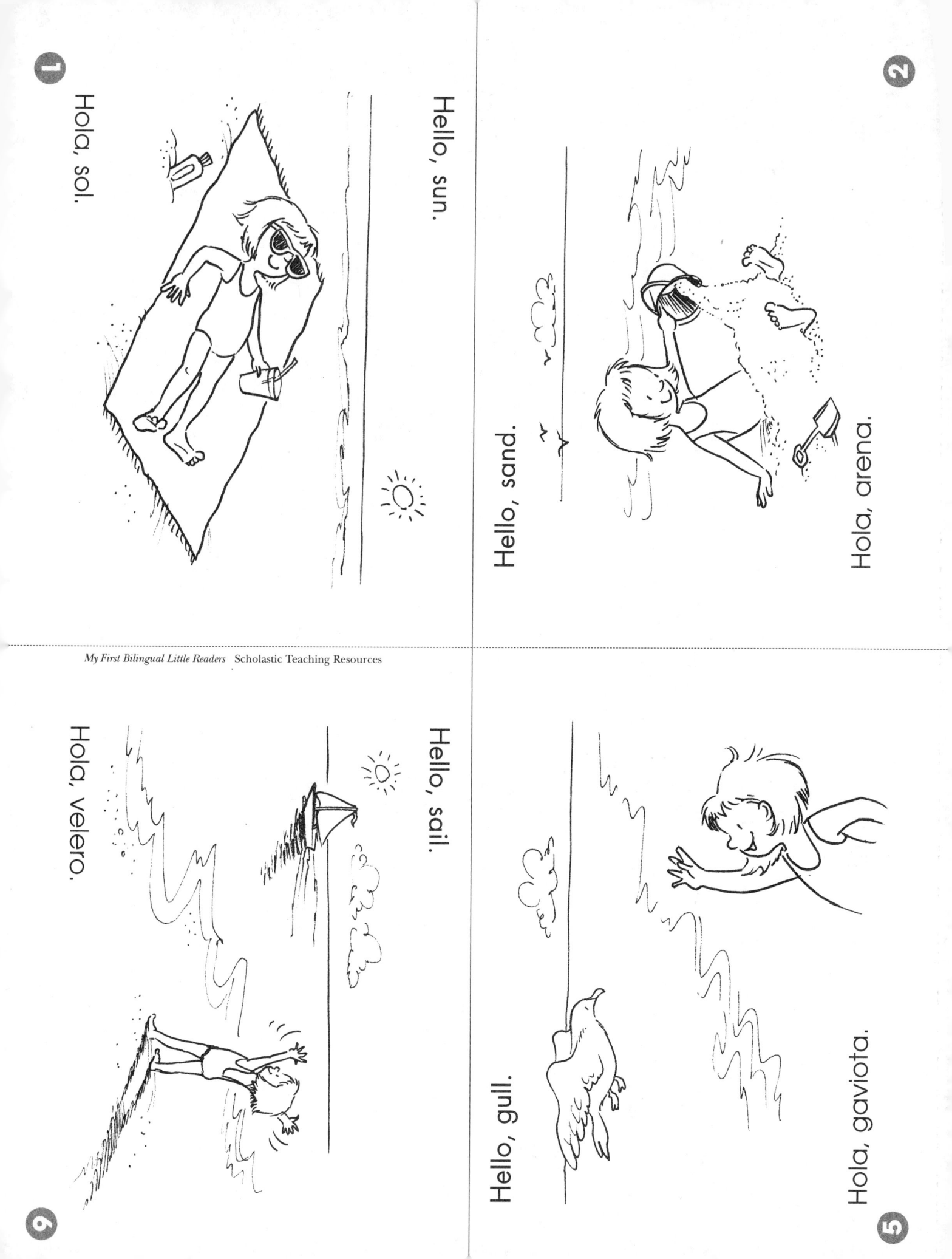

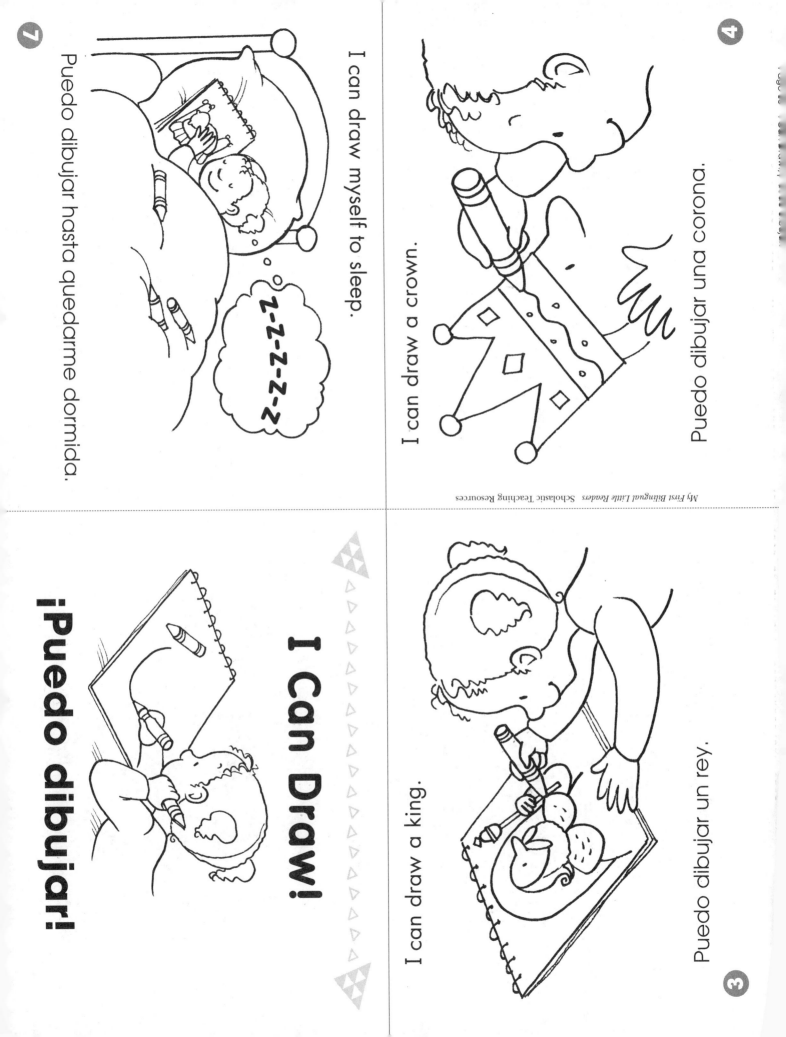

I can draw myself to sleep.

z-z-z-z

Puedo dibujar hasta quedarme dormida.

I can draw a crown.

Puedo dibujar una corona.

¡Puedo dibujar!

I Can Draw!

I can draw a king.

Puedo dibujar un rey.

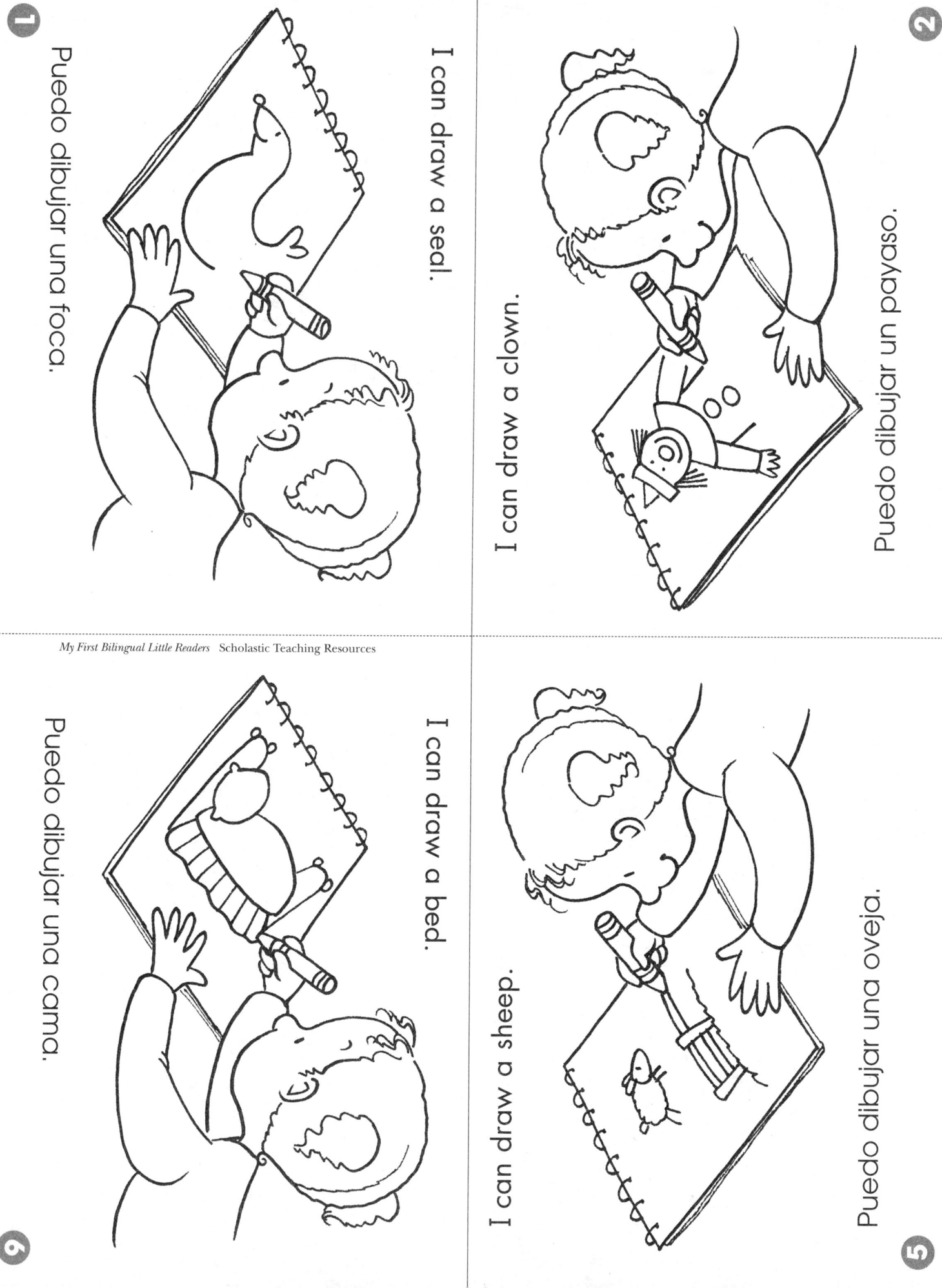

1

I can draw a seal.

Puedo dibujar una foca.

2

I can draw a clown.

Puedo dibujar un payaso.

6

I can draw a bed.

Puedo dibujar una cama.

5

I can draw a sheep.

Puedo dibujar una oveja.

Me puedo esconder detrás de mi pelo.

I can hide behind my hair.

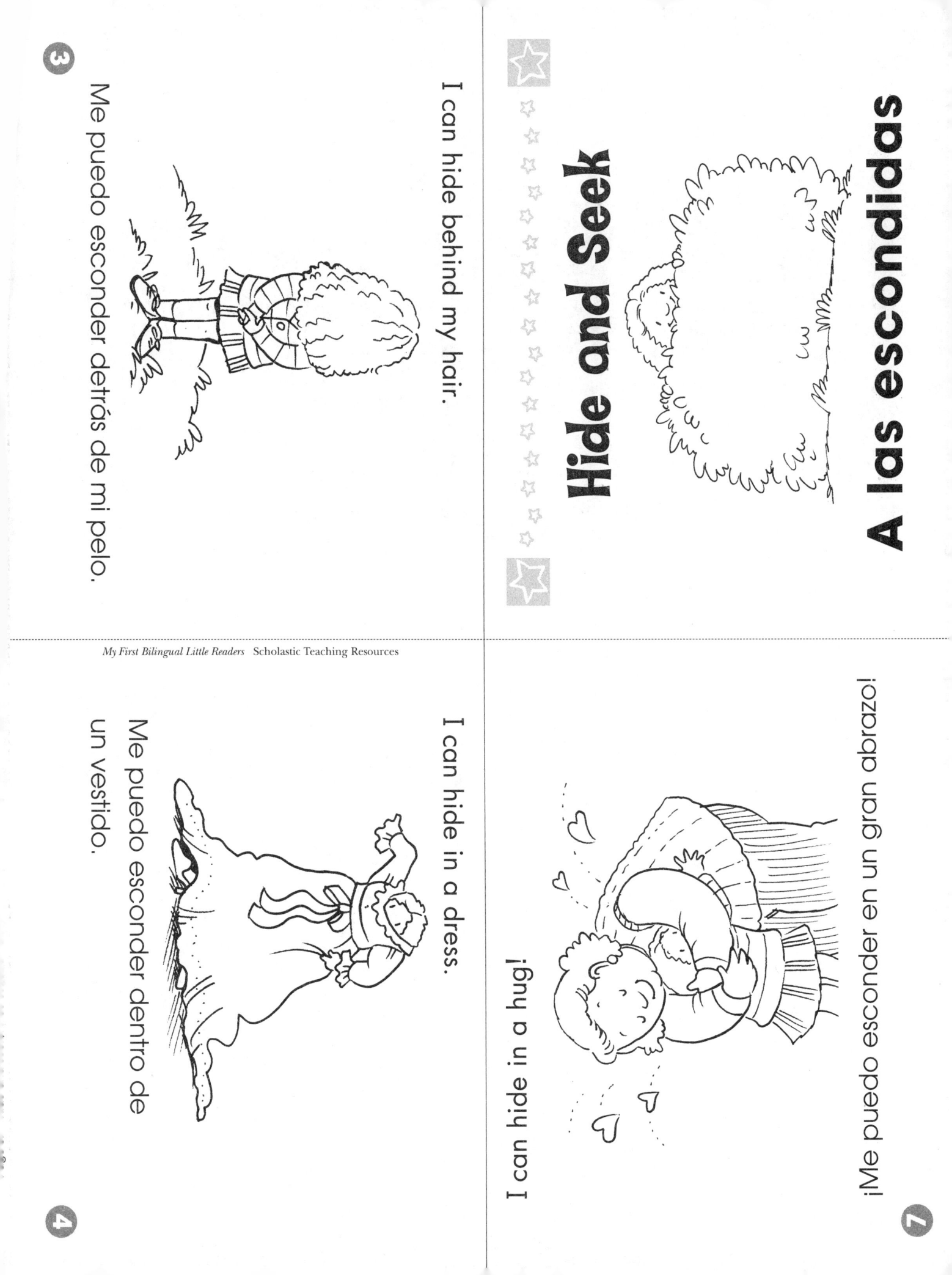

Hide and Seek

A las escondidas

Me puedo esconder dentro de un vestido.

I can hide in a dress.

I can hide in a hug!

¡Me puedo esconder en un gran abrazo!

Me puedo esconder debajo
de la alfombra.

I can hide under the rug.

Me puedo esconder en un lío de cosas.

I can hide in a mess.

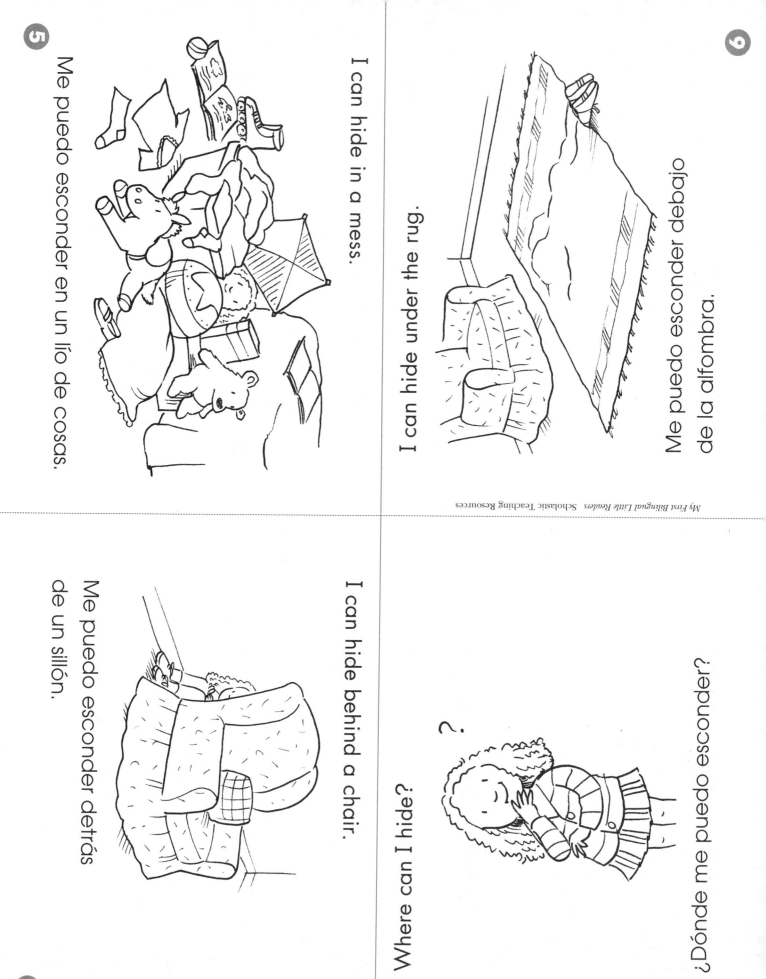

Me puedo esconder detrás
de un sillón.

I can hide behind a chair.

¿Dónde me puedo esconder?

Where can I hide?

Tengo un sombrero con agujeros.

I have a hat that has holes.

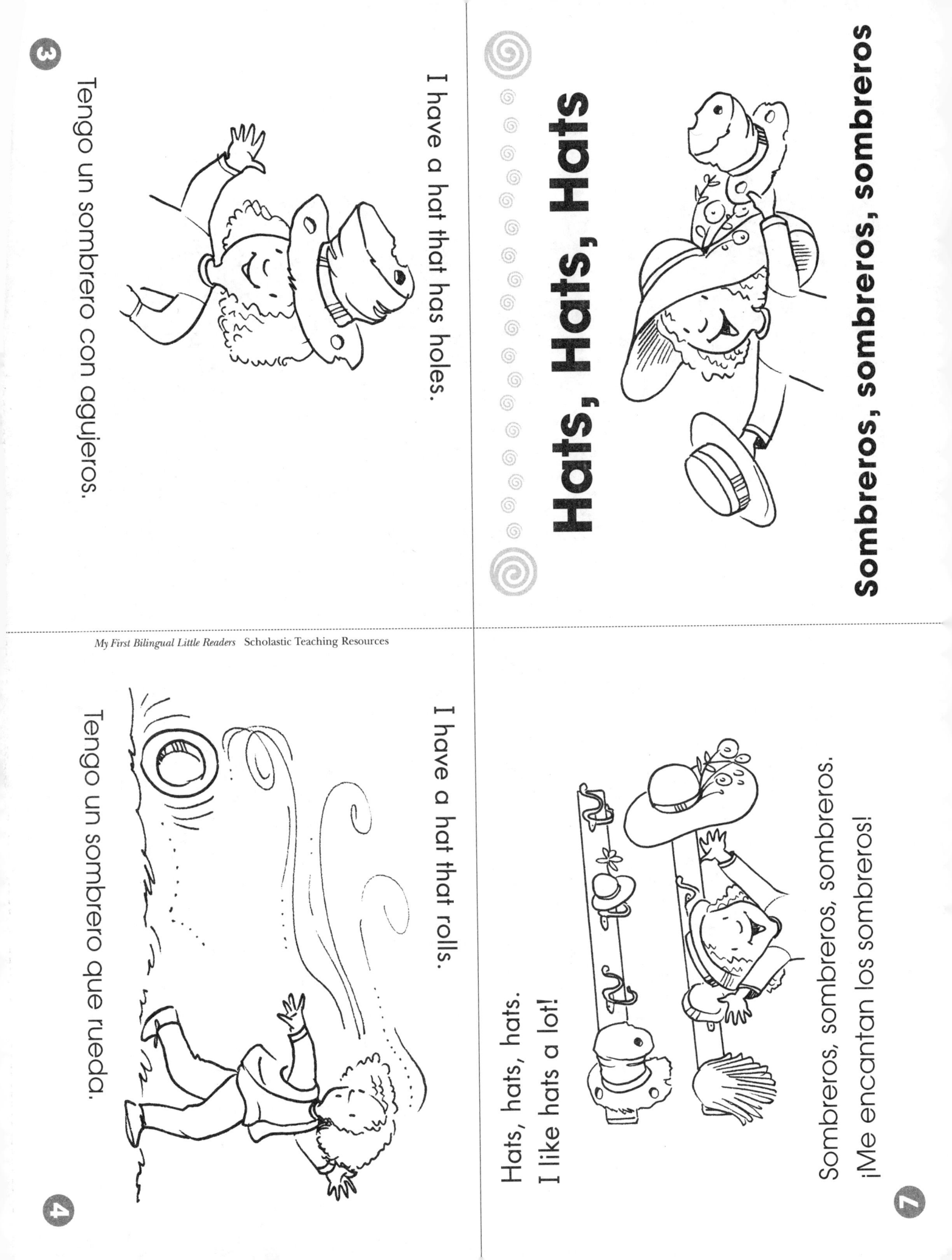

Hats, Hats, Hats

Sombreros, sombreros, sombreros

Tengo un sombrero que rueda.

I have a hat that rolls.

Hats, hats, hats.
I like hats a lot!

Sombreros, sombreros, sombreros.
¡Me encantan los sombreros!

6

I have a hat that is a mop.

Tengo un sombrero que es un trapeador.

5

I have a hat that flops.

Tengo un sombrero que se dobla.

1

I have a hat that is tall.

Tengo un sombrero alto.

2

I have a hat that is small.

Tengo un sombrero pequeño.

What Is for Supper?

¿Qué vamos a cenar?

I like tacos.

Me gustan los tacos.

3

I like grilled cheese.

Me gusta el queso.

4

I like to eat!

¡Me gusta comer!

7

5

I like fish sticks.

Me gustan las croquetas de pescado.

6

I like rice and beans.

Me gusta el arroz con frijoles.

2

I like pizza.

Me gusta la pizza.

1

I like pasta.

Me gusta la pasta.

¡Encontré seis cosas en total!

I found six things all together!

Encontré una piña.

I found a pine cone.

My First Bilingual Little Readers Scholastic Teaching Resources

¡Mira lo que encontré!

Look What I Found!

I found an acorn.

Encontré una bellota.

Encontré una hoja.

I found a leaf.

I found a feather.

Encontré una pluma.

Encontré una piedra.

I found a stone.

Look what I found!
I found a stick.

¡Mira lo que encontré!
Encontré un palo.